D1314958

Lawless

Colors by Val Staples

CRIMINAL VOL. 2: LAWLESS. Contains material originally published in magazine form as CRIMINAL #6-10. First printing 2007. ISBN# 978-0-7851-2816-8.
Published by MARVEL PUBLISHING. INC., a subsidiary of MARVEL ENTERTAINMENT INC. OFFICE OF PUBLICATION: 417 5th Avenue, New York, NY 10016.

Printed in Canada.

10 9 8 7 6 5 4 3 2 1

Lawless

A **CRIMINAL** edition by *Ed Brubaker* and *Sean Phillips*

Introduction

There you go again, Ed.

I mean, this getting a little old.

You flash a copy of your latest and I put it in my very large "to read soon" pile, some of which dates back to the Ford administration, and get on with my life.

So there I am, getting along with my life, which includes a tough deadline for an art job. I attack the art job with my usual zest, walking around the place and looking for something to read. I take a look at the "to read soon" pile. The letter from Herodotus crumbles when I pick it up, so I look your book over. I figure reading ten pages of Brubaker will put off my work for, well, ten pages.

Ten pages in I realize the art doesn't suck. Sure, I can tell from the start that this Sean can draw, but that alone does not make good comics. The text and art have to work together as intimately as lovers do, each serving the same purpose, each fully aware of the other's intent. The way Sean draws people getting shot is accurate: when struck by a bullet or a knuckle sandwich, you're not likely to fly twenty feet. Odds are you'll just sit down and look stupid. The relentless three-tier grid traps us in the hero's claustrophobic existential neighborhood. The effect is creepy. But then, you're a creep, Ed.

So this thing is definitely working. I keep reading.

Then your story starts unraveling all over the place and the heist yarn turns into a character study and the tough guy is revealed to be much more than just tough. A tight, smart crime and revenge story snaps along in quick chapters that make me think of a poker dealer thumbing a deck of cards. Everybody's an asshole, but I care about the worst of them. Two-thirds of the way in I'm certain the tough guy is going to wind up dead, but I have to stick around to see how fucked up the end is. And it's pretty random and fucked up. At least he gets laid, but somehow you manage to make that seem pretty random and fucked up too.

I'm working late tonight and won't get enough sleep, but at least I've read a damn good crime story.

Not many people really understand what makes a crime story tick. Like they did with the early Batman movies and with nearly every attempt at film noir since movies went to color, they dress it up dark, even murky, but the essential inner darkness that a good crime yarn exposes, relishes in, and releases never occurs to them. Your stuff is spot on, and wonderfully unforgiving. Best of all, it doesn't snicker at what it is, and it doesn't apologize for it, either.

One of these days I'll have to write you an introduction.

Frank Miller
New York City 2007

Living on the road my friend
Was gonna keep you free and clean
Now you wear your skin like iron
And your breath's as hard as kerosene

--Townes Van Zandt

Part One

GGGGKKKK...GG...

TRACY KNEW HE DIDN'T HAVE TO KILL HIM...

...BUT SOME PEOPLE JUST DESERVE TO DIE.

HE'D LEARNED THAT A LONG TIME AGO.

AND HE WAS OLD ENOUGH NOW THAT HE DIDN'T DOUBT HIS INSTINCTS.

EVEN WHEN THIS ONE HAD SEEN HIM COMING...

HEY, YOU'RE THAT GUY... SAM SOMEBODY?

WHAT THE FUCK DO YOU –

...HE DIDN'T HESITATE FOR A SECOND.

UOOFF!

IT WAS THE TIMING THAT MADE IT WORK.

BECAUSE THIS WASN'T LIKE OVERSEAS, WHERE YOU LEFT BODIES WHERE THEY FELL.

NOT UNLESS YOU WERE IN A HURRY, OR YOU WANTED TO SEND A MESSAGE.

AND TRACY WASN'T IN A HURRY THIS TIME. THERE WAS NO MESSAGE.

HE JUST WANTED THIS ASSHOLE TO DISAPPEAR

SO WHEN HE'D SEEN THIS DRUNKEN FOOL GO UP TO PISS OFF A ROOFTOP, AND SEEN THE GARBAGE TRUCKS ROLLING THROUGH THE SNOW-FILLED STREETS...

...IT HAD ALL CLICKED INTO PLACE.

HE'D BE ROTTING IN A LANDFILL BY MORNING, AND NO ONE WOULD EVEN KNOW.

AND NOW TRACY HAD A WAY IN.

HE'D ONLY BEEN BACK FOR TWO WEEKS, BUT HE ALREADY FELT THE FAMILIARITY SEEPING BACK INTO HIS BONES.

THE MEMORIES OF THE BACK ALLEYS AND TRAIN TRACKS RUNNING LIKE A VEIN THROUGH HIS MIND.

THIS WAS A HARD PLACE, A COLD PLACE.

IT FELT LIKE HOME.

WHEN HE WAS IN LOCK-UP, HE'D READ THOMAS WOLFE'S *YOU CAN'T GO HOME AGAIN.*

BUT TRACY THOUGHT THE TRUTH WAS YOU COULD NEVER REALLY LEAVE IT...

...NO MATTER HOW FAR OR HOW FAST YOU RAN.

WHAT -- WHAT THE FUCK IS THIS, TOP?

PERSONAL EFFECTS... *BRODERICK M. LAWLESS.*

ARRIVED FEBRUARY 10TH.

RICK...?

AFFIRMATIVE. YOU ARE THE ONLY *LIVING* RELATIVE, SO THEY SHIPPED THAT HERE.

FEBRUARY? IT'S NEARLY *DECEMBER.*

I KNOW THAT. BUT *YOU* KNOW WHAT THE *COLONEL* SAID.

NO *VISITORS,* NO *MAIL...* NO CONTACT WITH THE WORLD.

WE SAT ON A **SHIT-STORM** FOR YOU, LAWLESS.

DON'T FORGET THAT.

YOU MEAN, LOCKED ME AWAY UNTIL IT BLEW OVER ... DON'T YOU?

SEMANTICS.

EIGHTEEN MONTHS IN A **HOLE** IS A GIFT COMPARED TO WHAT YOU **COULD'VE** GOTTEN.

RIGHT.

THE ARMY AVOIDS A SCANDAL AND I GET TO KEEP MY JOB.

DON'T UNDERESTIMATE YOUR VALUE TO THIS UNIT.

SOMEONE SHOULD'VE TOLD ME.

IT WAS MY BROTHER

THAT'S THE DIFFERENCE BETWEEN YOU AND **ME**, LAWLESS. I FOLLOW **ORDERS.**

AND FROM WHAT I READ IN HIS FILE, YOUR LITTLE BROTHER WAS A **PIECE OF SHIT.**

THIEF, FELON, AND GENERALLY A BAD GUY.

I WOULDN'T CRY OVER IT IF I WERE YOU...

ANYWAY, HE'S LONG-BURIED BY NOW.

TWO NIGHTS LATER TRACY SLIPPED THROUGH A HOLE IN THE FENCE AND REJOINED THE WORLD.

HE SLEPT A LOT ON THE BUS, SPENDING HIS WAKING TIME THINKING ON WHAT HE'D NEED TO DO.

HIS MONEY WAS NEARLY GONE, AND HE'D NEED MORE BEFORE HE GOT TO THE CITY.

HE'D NEED A NEW NAME, TOO. A NEW I.D. AND A BACKGROUND THAT WOULD PASS A CURSORY CHECK.

LUCKILY, HE KNEW WHERE TO GO FOR THE LAST TWO.

THE MONEY, HE'D FIND ON THE WAY.

KNK KNNK

HANG ON'... I'M COMIN'...

WHAT'S THE *PROBLEM?* YOU DIDN'T SEE THE *SIGN* AT THE GATE?

HEY, JAKE... YOU LOOK TERRIBLE.

WHO THE FUCK ARE *YOU?* DO I KNOW...

JESUS FUCKING CHRIST.

TRACY?

YOU GONNA INVITE ME *IN,* OR SHOULD I START MAKIN' A *SNOWMAN* OUT HERE?

YEAH... UH, SURE... COME ON *IN.* IN.

WHAT THE HELL ARE *YOU* DOING IN THE CITY? WHAT'S IT BEEN... FIFTEEN YEARS?

MORE...

...AND WHY DO YOU *THINK* I'M HERE?

RICKY? THAT WAS ALMOST A *YEAR* AGO, MAN. AND I'M *LONG* OUT OF THAT WORLD.

I DON'T KNOW *ANYTHING* ABOUT THAT.

I DIDN'T COME TO *YOU* FOR ANSWERS, JACOB.

I CAME FOR WHAT YOU DO *BEST*.

WHAT? NO. I DON'T *DO THAT* ANYMORE. I HAVEN'T FOR YEARS.

WHICH IS WHY THIS IS GOING TO WORK.

YOU'RE ONE OF MAYBE FIVE PEOPLE IN THE CITY WHO EVEN *MIGHT* RECOGNIZE ME, AND YOU DIDN'T.

IF I'M GOING TO FIND OUT ABOUT MY BROTHER, I NEED TO TAKE ADVANTAGE OF THAT.

SO THIS IS SOME KIND OF FAVOR? LIKE YOU AND ME WERE *EVER* FRIENDS?

NO. BUT I'M NOT BLIND...

...YOU COULD *CLEARLY* USE THE *MONEY*.

CHRIST, WHAT WERE YOU *DOING* OVER THERE? RAIDING SADDAM'S PALACES?

THE MONEY HAD COME TO HIM THE DAY BEFORE IN *CENTER CITY*, DURING A STOPOVER ON THE GREYHOUND.

TRACY REMEMBERED HIS FATHER RANTING ABOUT THE CENTER CITY *DOCKS* BEING A PLACE A LOT OF *CASH* LEFT THE COUNTRY TO BE LAUNDERED.

HE HOPED THAT WAS STILL THE CASE TWENTY YEARS LATER

A FEW HOURS LATER, HE FOUND OUT THIS PORT WAS A TWO-WAY STREET.

EVEN AFTER ALL HIS TIME AWAY FROM THE LIFE, HE COULD TELL WHEN SOMEONE WAS CARRYING SOMEONE *ELSE'S* MONEY FOR DELIVERY.

BUT THEN, THOSE WERE THE KIND OF OBSERVATION SKILLS THAT HAD MADE HIM SO VALUABLE TO THE ARMY.

HEY -- HOLD ON.

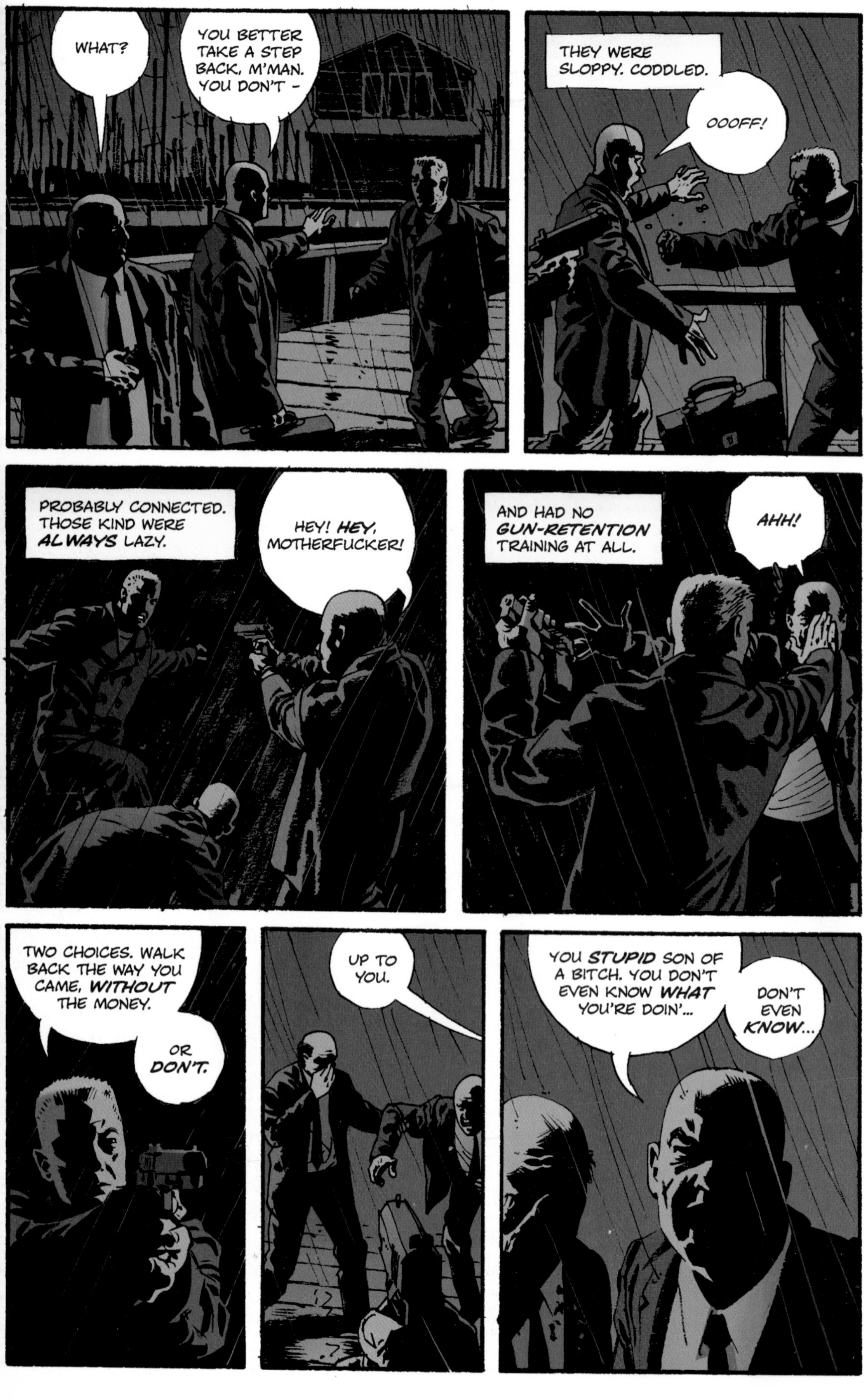
WHAT?
YOU BETTER TAKE A STEP BACK, M'MAN. YOU DON'T -
THEY WERE SLOPPY. CODDLED.
OOOFF!
PROBABLY CONNECTED. THOSE KIND WERE ALWAYS LAZY.
HEY! HEY, MOTHERFUCKER!
AND HAD NO GUN-RETENTION TRAINING AT ALL.
AHH!
TWO CHOICES. WALK BACK THE WAY YOU CAME, WITHOUT THE MONEY.
OR DON'T.
UP TO YOU.
YOU STUPID SON OF A BITCH. YOU DON'T EVEN KNOW WHAT YOU'RE DOIN'...
DON'T EVEN KNOW...

I HAVE A PRETTY GOOD IDEA.

YOU MAKE THAT *CHOICE* YET?

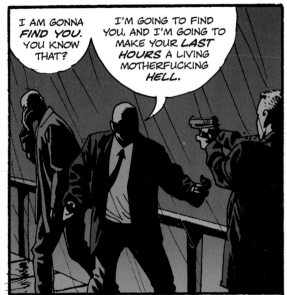

I AM GONNA *FIND YOU.* YOU KNOW THAT?

I'M GOING TO FIND YOU, AND I'M GOING TO MAKE YOUR *LAST HOURS* A LIVING MOTHERFUCKING *HELL.*

I GUESS I BELIEVE YOU.

JESUS!

BE *SMARTER* THAN YOUR FRIEND.

OKAY... OKAY...

THE NEXT BUS LEFT IN AN HOUR

HE'D BE LONG GONE BEFORE WHOEVER'S *MONEY* THIS WAS MOBILIZED HIS PEOPLE TO LOOK FOR IT.

HE'D MOVED QUICKLY, AND STAYED IN THE SHADOWS, SO HE WASN'T WORRIED ABOUT HAVING BEEN SEEN.

NO ONE KNEW WHO HE *WAS* ANYMORE, AND BESIDES, THIS WAS JUST A *STOPOVER.*

FAAASH!

THAT A GOOD ONE?

IT'S AN I.D. PHOTO, TRACY... IT'S NOT *SUPPOSED* TO BE.

SO, ON THE FORM, THIS IS WHO YOU WANT TO BE - *SAM WEST*?

YEAH, HOW LONG TO GET A FEW CREDIT CARDS, TOO?

I'LL HAVE TO MAKE A CALL.

COULD TAKE A FEW DAYS, IF YOU WANT SOMETHING THAT'LL CLEAR A *BACKGROUND*.

I DO. THIS HAS TO BE *REAL*. AND I'M GONNA NEED A *PERSONAL REFERENCE*, TOO.

SOMEONE WHO I "WORKED WITH" SOMETIME.

THAT COULD BE TOUGHER

I'LL FIGURE IT OUT.

RIGHT NOW, THOUGH, I NEED TO HEAR ABOUT *RICKY*.

LIKE I SAID, I'M *NOT* PART OF THAT WORLD. I WASN'T TIGHT WITH HIM *OR* HIS PEOPLE.

HADN'T EVEN *SEEN HIM* FOR FOUR OR FIVE YEARS WHEN I HEARD HE WAS DEAD.

SURE, BUT YOU'RE NOT A *VIRGIN*, JACOB.

YOU AT LEAST KNOW *SOMEONE* WHO WAS ON HIS CREW...

THERE'S NO GUARANTEE ANY OF THEM WILL SHOW UP TONIGHT...

THEN WE COME BACK TOMORROW.

I HAVE A *LIFE*, Y'KNOW?

THAT'S A *GENEROUS* DESCRIPTION OF WHAT YOU HAVE, JACOB.

FUCK YOU.

NOW THERE'S THE *OLD* JAKE.

WHAT DID THEY *DO* TO YOU?

NONE OF YOUR --

THERE.

THAT GUY?

YEAH. NAME'S *GRAY* SOMETHING OR OTHER

HE WAS PART OF RICKY'S STRING.

AND SO'S THE GIRL... THAT'S *MALLORY*.

SHE WAS RICKY'S *GIRL*, MOST OF THE TIME.

NOW GET THE FUCK OUT OF MY CAR

THE UNDERTOWN BAR HAD BEEN CALLED *THE UNDERTOW* FOR AS LONG AS TRACY COULD REMEMBER

THE LAST N ON THE NEON SIGN HAD BURNED OUT SOMETIME IN THE 50S AND NEVER BEEN FIXED.

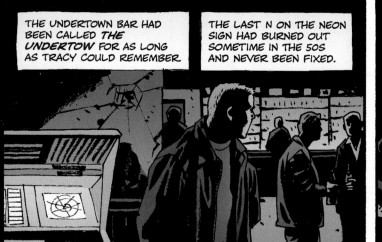

THOUGH HE KNEW THE PLACE, TRACY HAD NEVER BEEN A REGULAR. THIS WAS HIS FATHER'S BAR.

ALTHOUGH HIS DAD SPENT HALF HIS TIME 86'D FROM IT FOR FIGHTING.

APPARENTLY, AS THE OLD-TIMERS GOT SENT AWAY OR BURIED, THE NEXT GENERATION HAD TAKEN THEIR SEATS AT THE BAR

BECAUSE THE PLACE WAS STILL THRIVING, AND *STILL* FILLED WITH CRIMINALS.

GNARLY WAS STILL BEHIND THE BAR, BUT IF HE RECOGNIZED TRACY, HE DIDN'T LET ON.

WHATEVER'S *DARK* ON TAP.

COMIN' UP.

THE LITTLE KID BUSSING TABLES WAS STRANGE, EVEN FOR THE UNDERTOW.

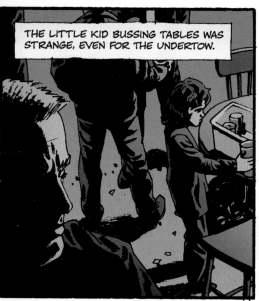

BUT THE CUSTOMERS TREATED HER LIKE SHE OWNED THE PLACE.

USE AN *ASHTRAY*, CURTIS!

ALRIGHT, ANGIE, *ALRIGHT...* SORRY...

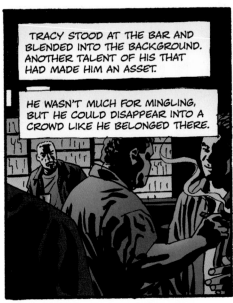

TRACY STOOD AT THE BAR AND BLENDED INTO THE BACKGROUND. ANOTHER TALENT OF HIS THAT HAD MADE HIM AN ASSET.

HE WASN'T MUCH FOR MINGLING, BUT HE COULD DISAPPEAR INTO A CROWD LIKE HE BELONGED THERE.

AFTER A FEW DRINKS MALLORY AND GRAY WERE JOINED BY TWO OTHER MEN...

DAVEY... WHAT THE *FUCK?* YOU'RE LATE.

WE ON A *CLOCK* ALL OF A SUDDEN?

THE WAY THEY HUDDLED TOGETHER IN THE BOOTH, IT WAS CLEAR THIS WAS THE CREW...

RICKY'S OLD CREW.

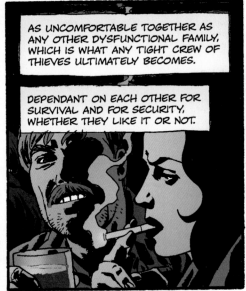

AS UNCOMFORTABLE TOGETHER AS ANY OTHER DYSFUNCTIONAL FAMILY, WHICH IS WHAT ANY TIGHT CREW OF THIEVES ULTIMATELY BECOMES.

DEPENDANT ON EACH OTHER FOR SURVIVAL AND FOR SECURITY, WHETHER THEY LIKE IT OR NOT.

THE THOUGHT THAT SOMEONE IN THIS CREW, ONE OF HIS *FAMILY*, HAD LEFT RICK FACE-DOWN IN AN ALLEY FLIPPED A SWITCH IN TRACY'S MIND.

HE STOPPED SEEING THEM AS PEOPLE, BUT AS TARGETS, INSTEAD.

STILL, THERE WERE ANSWERS THAT HAD TO COME BEFORE THAT... PATIENCE.

THE THING THE ARMY TEACHES BEST. THE ART OF WAITING.

SO HE WAITED AND WATCHED...

...AND THOUGHT ABOUT THE LAST TIME HE'D BEEN IN A BAR, NEARLY TWO YEARS BEFORE.

IN BAGHDAD, THE GREEN ZONE.

THE *ENLISTED CLUB* HAD ONCE BEEN A RESTAURANT, BUT IT DIDN'T SERVE ANYTHING BUT BOOZE AND STALE CHIPS ANYMORE.

STILL, IT WAS A PLACE TO BLOW OFF STEAM, AWAY FROM THE HOSTILES.

NOT THAT THERE WASN'T STILL PLENTY OF HOSTILITY TO GO AROUND.

--AN' THIS LITTLE BITCH EYES JUST GLARE AT ME FROM OUTTA' HER FUCKIN' VEIL...

SO I GRAB THAT SHIT. I PULL IT BACK AND SHOW THE WORLD HER FUCKIN' FACE.

EXPOSED.

SHOULDA' SEEN IT. HER FATHER GOES BA-FUCKIN'-LISTIC.

STARTS SCREAMIN' IN SAND-NIGGER... TOTAL CRACK-UP.

TRACY AND HIS UNIT WEREN'T HERE FOR THIS SHIT, HOLDING BACK A NEVER-ENDING TIDE.

THEY WERE ON SPECIAL DETAIL. ONE WEEK, IN AND OUT.

IF HE HADN'T PICKED THIS ONE NIGHT TO BLEND IN, GET A FEEL FOR THE TERRITORY AND THE SOLDIERS HERE...

THING IS — LISTEN TA' THIS — THING IS, TH' LITTLE BITCH IS *HOT FER TEACHER.*

SWEET VIRGIN TITTIES, LIKE FRESH FRUIT. *RIPE.*

YOU '*MEMBER* FRUIT? WHAT'RE YOU, GAY?

HEY — *DON'T ASK, DON'T TELL!*

BWAA HA HA!

SHOW YOU HOW FUCKIN' GAY I AM... BASTARDS...

...MAYBE THINGS WOULD HAVE BEEN DIFFERENT.

FOR HIM, AT LEAST.

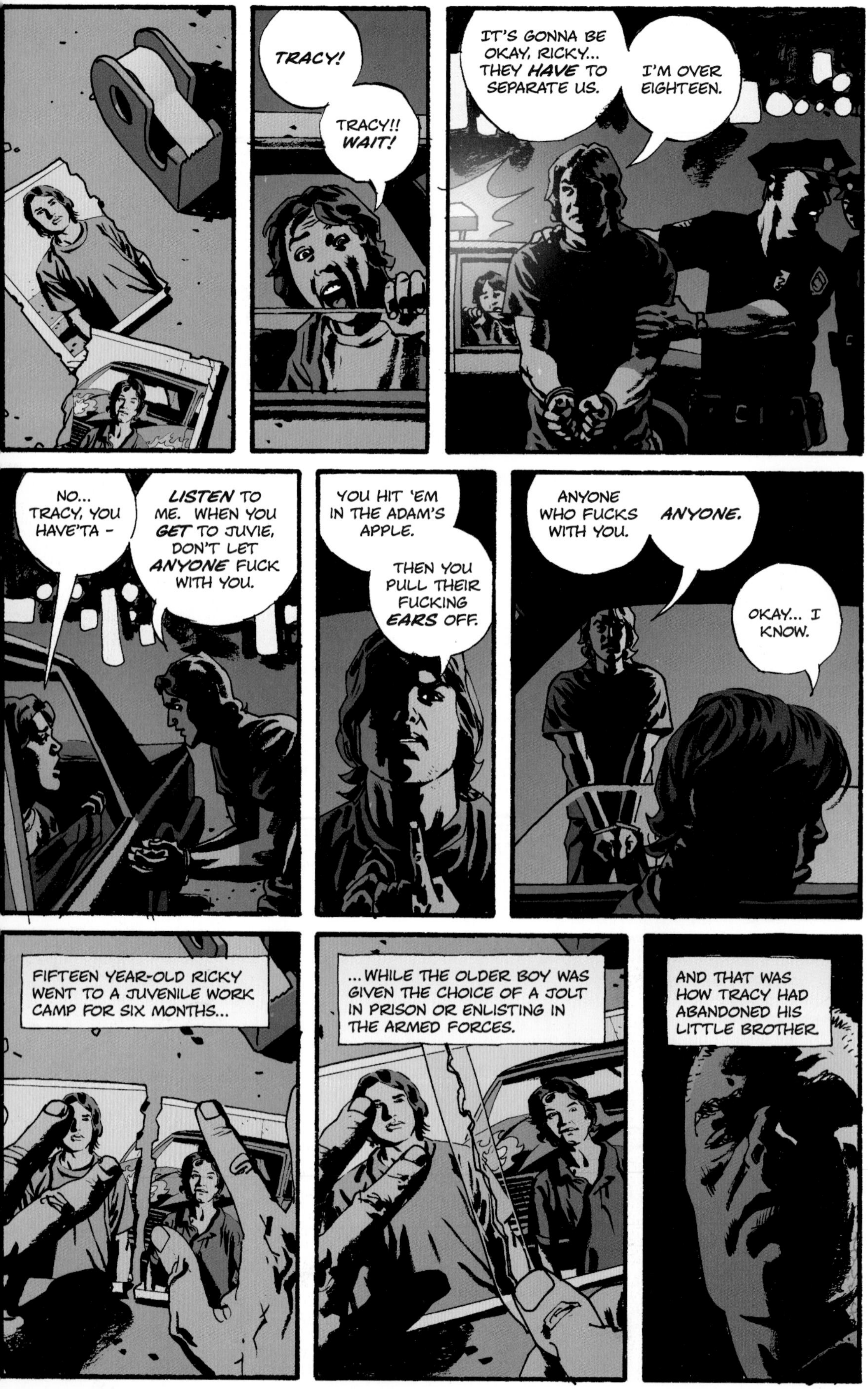
TRACY!
TRACY!! WAIT!
IT'S GONNA BE OKAY, RICKY... THEY HAVE TO SEPARATE US.
I'M OVER EIGHTEEN.
NO... TRACY, YOU HAVE'TA -
LISTEN TO ME. WHEN YOU GET TO JUVIE, DON'T LET ANYONE FUCK WITH YOU.
YOU HIT 'EM IN THE ADAM'S APPLE.
THEN YOU PULL THEIR FUCKING EARS OFF.
ANYONE WHO FUCKS WITH YOU.
ANYONE.
OKAY... I KNOW.
FIFTEEN YEAR-OLD RICKY WENT TO A JUVENILE WORK CAMP FOR SIX MONTHS...
...WHILE THE OLDER BOY WAS GIVEN THE CHOICE OF A JOLT IN PRISON OR ENLISTING IN THE ARMED FORCES.
AND THAT WAS HOW TRACY HAD ABANDONED HIS LITTLE BROTHER.

OR AT LEAST, THAT WAS HOW HE THOUGHT OF IT OVER THE YEARS.

THAT HE CHOSE HIS OWN ESCAPE, AND LEFT RICKY IN THEIR FATHER'S WORLD... IN THEIR FATHER'S HOUSE.

HE WAS A TOUGH KID, TRACY HAD TOLD HIMSELF, HE'D SURVIVE.

EVEN GET TOUGHER, MOST LIKELY.

AND FROM WHAT HE'D READ IN RICKY'S FILE, BOTH THOSE THINGS WERE TRUE.

UNTIL NEITHER OF THEM WERE.

YOU **DONE?**

I HAVE DEADLINES.

HE SPENT THE NEXT WEEK AND A HALF CREATING A LIFE FOR HIS NEW NAME.

HE USED *MOST* OF THE MONEY HE HAD LEFT TO BUY A FAST CAR

AND HE CASHED IN A LONG-OVERDUE FAVOR TO PAD OUT HIS REPUTATION.

THEN HE DID JUST ENOUGH TO GET HIS NAME – SAM WEST – KNOWN TO THE RIGHT PEOPLE.

YEAH, DID A LITTLE *DRIVING* UP NORTH.

I'LL LET YOU KNOW IF I HEAR ANYTHING.

DOESN'T *HAVE* TO BE SOMETHING HEAVY...

I'M JUST LOOKING FOR SOME *PICK-UP.*

RICKY'S OLD CREW WERE MEETING ALMOST EVERY NIGHT, AND THE WAY THEY ACTED REMINDED HIM OF HIS DAD'S GANG...

...WHENEVER THEY WERE ABOUT TO TAKE DOWN A SCORE.

SO, IF HIS PLAN WAS GOING TO WORK, HE HAD TO MOVE SOON.

LATER, DAVEY... AND GET SOME *SLEEP* FOR A CHANGE.

SLEEP IS FOR *PUSSIES!* HA HA HA...

HE'D CHOSEN THIS ONE - DAVEY - AS THE WEAKEST LINK THE FIRST TIME HE'D SEEN THEM.

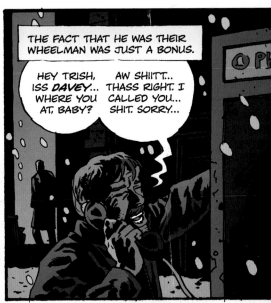

THE FACT THAT HE WAS THEIR WHEELMAN WAS JUST A BONUS.

HEY TRISH, ISS *DAVEY*... WHERE YOU AT, BABY?

AW SHIITT... THASS RIGHT. I CALLED YOU... SHIT. SORRY...

WELL, FUCK HER... DON'EED HER...

HE FELT LIKE A PREDATOR...

...A SILENT HUNTER...

...AS HE PONDERED HIS OPTIONS.

HOW TO BEST GET THIS *DAVEY* OUT OF THE WAY, SO HIS CREW WOULD NEED A NEW RECRUIT.

AND THEN DAVEY MADE THE DECISION FOR HIM.

PAY YOU? FER WHAAAT?

AW *NO*... DON'T YOU EVEN *START* TO TRY TO –

WHAT'RE *YOU* GONNA DO, BITCH?

CALL'A COPS?!

NAA--

KRAKK

HE BROKE THE GIRL'S NOSE, AND PROBABLY BRUISED SOME RIBS.

LEFT HER CRYING IN THE BACK OF A TAXI...

...WHILE HE WENT UP TO THE ROOFTOP OF HIS OWN BUILDING...

...TO EMPTY HIS BLADDER ON THE CITY BELOW...

...AND TRACY NOTICED THE GARBAGE TRUCKS.

AFTER THAT, HE WOULDN'T HAVE LONG TO WAIT.

DAVEY WAS A FLAKE, BUT HIS COMPLETE ABSENCE WOULD BE UNUSUAL. DISTURBING.

ESPECIALLY WITH A JOB IN THE WORKS.

HE SAW THAT THE NEXT NIGHT, AS DAVEY'S PEOPLE QUICKLY WENT FROM ANNOYED TO ANGRY...

ASSHOLE PROBABLY FOUND SOMEWHERE TO GET HIS *DICK STINKY* AND FELL IN...

AND HE NOTICED GRAY CALCULATING WHAT THIS MEANT FOR THEIR PLANS.

CALL HIM AGAIN, NELSON.

HE AIN'T PICKIN' UP, MAN. GOES STRAIGHT TO MESSAGE.

I *WARNED YOU* ABOUT COUNTING ON HIM.

HE HASN'T BEEN RIGHT SINCE... SHIT, MAYBE *EVER.*

SHUT UP, MAL... ALL RIGHT?

JUST LET ME THINK.

AND IN A FEW DAYS, RUMORS OF DAVEY'S DISAPPEARANCE WERE ALL OVER THE GRAPEVINE...

FOUND SOME RICH *COOZE* AND WENT ON A *BENDER* DOWN TA CALI.

CALLED HALEY'S *DAUGHTER* FROM *VEGAS*, OUT OF HIS MIND ON METH ...

WELL, I HEARD HYDE'S BOYS PICKED HIM UP... PROBABLY *DESERVED IT*, TOO.

VICIOUS LITTLE FUCK.

AND TRACY KNEW, IT WAS TIME TO MAKE HIS MOVE.

YOU WANT TO BE THE ONE TO PASS THAT ALONG TO SIMON?

CAUSE I DON'T, GRAY.

FOR ALL WE KNOW, DAVEY'S BEEN PICKED UP BY THE COPS.

NO. I TOLD YOU, GNARLY LOOKED INTO THAT FOR ME.

DAVEY'S IN THE WIND, THAT'S ALL. LOST HIS NERVE, YET AGAIN.

OR FELL INTO A BOTTLE, *YET AGAIN.*

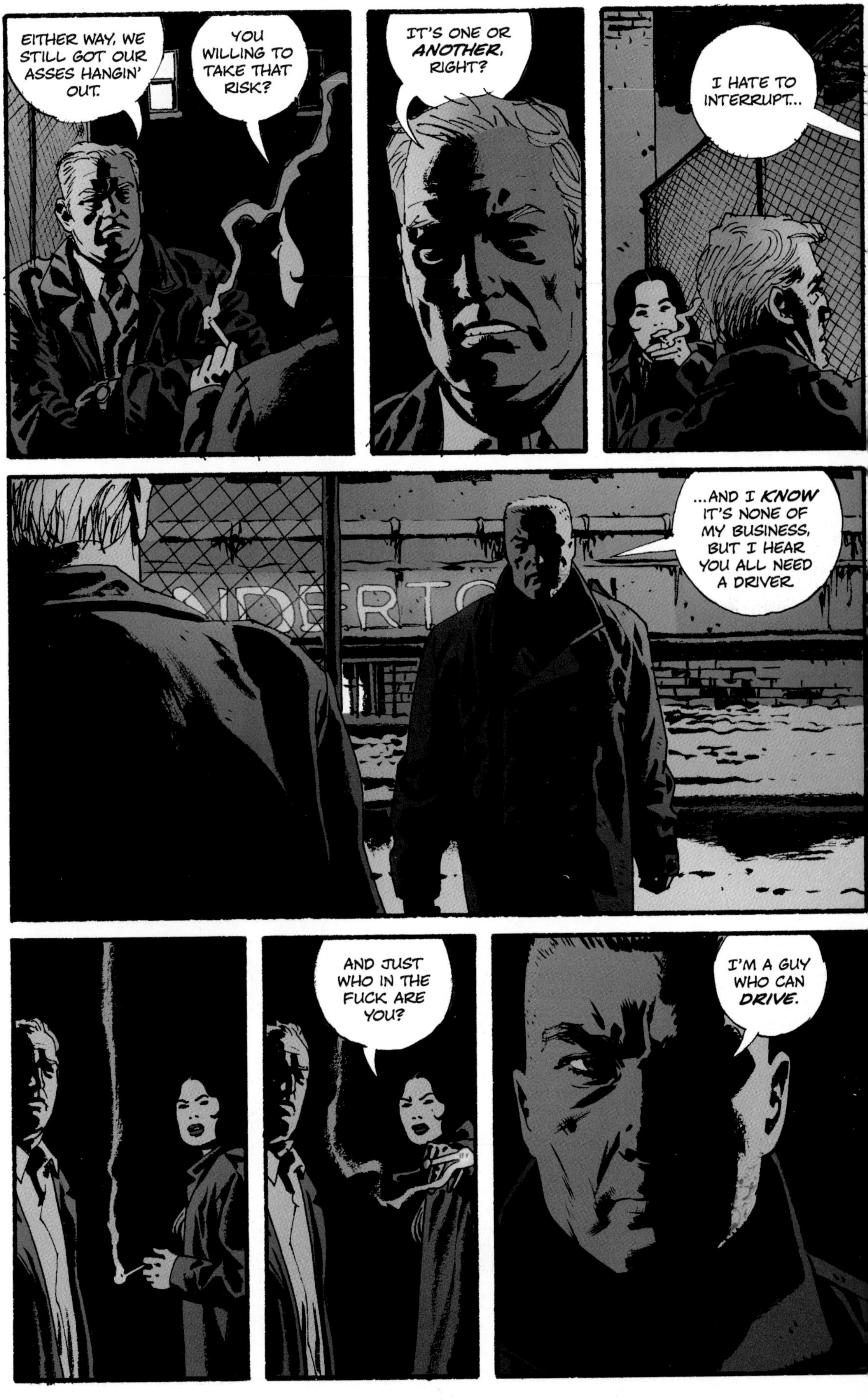
EITHER WAY, WE STILL GOT OUR ASSES HANGIN' OUT.
YOU WILLING TO TAKE THAT RISK?
IT'S ONE OR ANOTHER, RIGHT?
I HATE TO INTERRUPT...
...AND I KNOW IT'S NONE OF MY BUSINESS, BUT I HEAR YOU ALL NEED A DRIVER
AND JUST WHO IN THE FUCK ARE YOU?
I'M A GUY WHO CAN DRIVE.

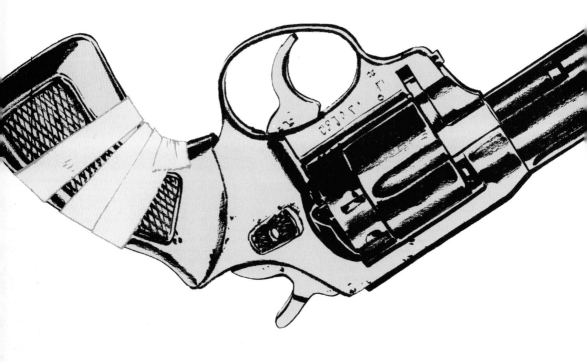

Part Two

HE KNEW HE HAD TO IMPRESS HER...

...AND HE COULD TELL MALLORY DIDN'T IMPRESS EASILY.

IS THERE ANYTHING *OTHER* THAN A.M.?

SO, THE POLICE CAR TRACY CUT-OFF WHEN HE RAN THE RED LIGHT?

SKREEEE

THAT WAS *MOSTLY* FOR HER BENEFIT.

WHEEOOO-WHEEEOOOO

ARE YOU *RETARDED*?

I CAN'T DITCH A *COP*, WHAT USE AM I?

THOUGHT YOU WANTED TO SEE HOW *GOOD* I WAS?

SURE... I'D JUST RATHER *NOT GET ARRESTED* FINDING OUT.

I'LL MAKE YOU A DEAL. IF WE GET *BUSTED*...

...YOU DON'T HAVE TO HIRE ME.

UH HUNH.

SO, YOU GONNA OPEN THIS THING *UP*, OR WHAT?

ABSOLUTELY.

TRACY WASN'T SOME KIND OF CAR FANATIC OR GEAR-HEAD, BUT HE KNEW WHAT HE LIKED.

AND HIS WHOLE LIFE, HE'D LIKED THE DODGE CHARGER

VRROOOOMMMMM

FAST, SLICK, AND YOU DIDN'T NEED A COMPUTER TO TUNE IT UP.

MY FRIEND, YOU LOOK LIKE A MAN WHO *KNOWS* HIS CARS.

$24999

AND NOT SO HARD TO COME BY THAT THERE WEREN'T STILL PLENTY ON THE ROAD.

$24999

I KNOW *THIS* CAR

THAT WAS IMPORTANT IN A GETAWAY CAR, THAT IT NOT *COMPLETELY* STAND OUT IN A CROWD.

THEN MY WORK HERE IS *DONE*, ISN'T IT?

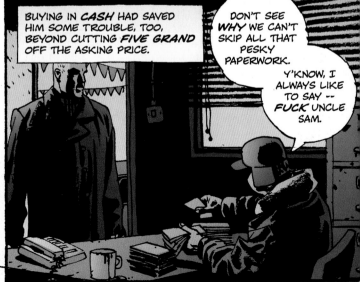

BUYING IN *CASH* HAD SAVED HIM SOME TROUBLE, TOO, BEYOND CUTTING *FIVE GRAND* OFF THE ASKING PRICE.

DON'T SEE *WHY* WE CAN'T SKIP ALL THAT PESKY PAPERWORK.

Y'KNOW, I ALWAYS LIKE TO SAY -- *FUCK* UNCLE SAM.

AND IT HANDLED WELL.

ALMOST LIKE THE ONE HIS FATHER HAD TAUGHT HIM TO DRIVE WITH.

HEY!!

JESUS!

FUCK!

WOULD YOU *RELAX?* I'M WORKING HERE.

WHEEEOOO WHEEOOO

WHY ARE **ALL** WHEELMEN INSANE? CAN YOU TELL ME THAT?

I'M NOT A SHRINK, SO I DON'T KNOW.

YEAH. I GUESS NOT...

OKAY, YOU'RE IN FOR THIS ONE JOB, AS LONG AS YOUR **REFERENCE** CHECKS OUT.

NOW GET US BACK TO **GRAY** BEFORE THAT IDIOT CIRCLES BACK.

HE WASN'T WORRIED ABOUT HIS REFERENCE. HE'D TAKEN CARE OF THAT THE DAY AFTER HE BOUGHT THE CAR.

SAM WEST? AM I SUPPOSED TO *KNOW* YOU?

YES AND NO.

COUNTY JAIL

DO NOT TOUCH THE GLASS!

LEO PATTERSON HAD BEEN HIS BROTHER'S BEST FRIEND WHEN THEY WERE KIDS.

TRACY REMEMBERED HIM AS BOTH SMART AND CAREFUL...

...AND WAS GLAD TO SEE AT LEAST *THAT* HADN'T CHANGED.

IT'S BEEN A LONG TIME, "SAM"... A *REALLY* LONG TIME.

I KNOW...AND THIS *ISN'T* WHERE I EXPECTED YOU TO BE...

WITH SIX *BODIES* HANGING OVER YOU.

MY LAWYER SAYS MOST OF THAT'S GONNA GET *TOSSED* BEFORE TRIAL...

BUT YOU'RE NOT HERE TO *CATCH UP*, ARE YOU "SAM?"

NO. I NEED YOUR HELP.

I HESITATE TO POINT OUT THE OBVIOUS...?

IT'S SOMETHING YOU CAN DO FROM IN HERE.

DO NOT TOUCH THE GLASS!

WHAT?

SAY WE WORKED TOGETHER IN *SANTA TERESA*, THAT I'M A GOOD DRIVER

SAY THIS TO *WHO*?

I DON'T KNOW. SOMEONE'LL GET IN TOUCH.

I'M GUESSING NO ONE FINDS OUT YOUR *REAL NAME* IN THIS SCENARIO?

IF THEY *DO*, IT'LL NEVER COME BACK TO YOU.

OKAY, THEN.

ALL RIGHT.

THIS IS ABOUT *RICKY*?

YEAH. I'M HERE TO FIND OUT THE TRUTH.

THAT'S...UH... THAT'S PROBABLY NOT SUCH A GREAT IDEA.?

HE *WASN'T* THE KID YOU REMEMBER

AND WHOSE FAULT IS THAT?

WHAT, *YOURS*? SHIT. MIGHT AS WELL BLAME THE WORLD.

NO... I SHOULD'VE DONE WHAT *YOU* DID, LEO. TAKEN CARE OF MY FATHER

BUT THAT DIDN'T *HELP*, DID IT?

ALL I DID WAS SCREW UP EVERYONE'S LIVES EVEN *WORSE* THAN THEY ALREADY WERE...

THEN I SHOULD'VE COME HOME.

MAYBE, BUT LOOK... WE BOTH KNOW RICKY NEVER HAD A CHANCE...

...HE JUST... HE WASN'T LIKE YOU.

POP

WELL, ALL RIGHT, LITTLE RICKY...

...LOOKS LIKE WE'RE GONNA MAKE A *MAN* OUTTA YOU, AFTER ALL.

IT'S DEAD... OH... OH.

I DON'T *FEEL GOOD*, DADDY... I WANNA GO HOME.

WHAT?! ARE YOU — *GOD DAMN IT!*

YOU LITTLE *FUCKIN' CRYBABY!*

WAIT! *WAIT!* DADDY — NO, I —

HIS FATHER'S IDEA OF TARGET PRACTICE. SHOOTING BIRDS ON THE CITY'S ROOFTOPS.

TRACY WOULD NEVER FORGET THE TREMOR IN HIS LITTLE BROTHER'S VOICE THAT DAY, AFTER HIS FIRST KILL.

HIS HEART CLEARLY *BROKEN* BY THE SAD, LONESOME DEATH OF A PIGEON.

POP

FOR HIS PART, TRACY FELT NOTHING.

HE'D BEEN ON THESE ROOFTOPS WITH DAD BEFORE AND DEATH DIDN'T PHASE HIM.

CERTAINLY NOT THE DEATH OF A BIRD.

POP

SO HE KEPT SHOOTING... HOPING TO WIPE OUT THE SOUND OF HIS BROTHER'S CRYING.

POP

POP

POP

WHAT I STILL DON'T GET IS WHY YOU THINK *THEY* KILLED RICKY?

I MEAN, THEY WERE HIS *PARTNERS*... RIGHT?

A THIEF IS *JUST* AS LIKELY TO BE KILLED BY ONE OF THEIR OWN CREW.

YOU SHOULD KNOW *THAT*, JAKE.

OR WEREN'T YOU PAYING ATTENTION TO OUR PARENTS AT ALL?

SOMETIMES I FEEL LIKE THAT'S *ALL* I DID... PAY ATTENTION TO THOSE ASSHOLES.

THOUGHT THEY WERE SO COOL. I USED TO SIT ON THE BASEMENT STAIRS AND LISTEN TO THEM...

PLANNING THEIR JOBS, ARGUING, SMOKING... ALWAYS *SO* DANGEROUS, RIGHT?

THEY WERE *THAT*, FOR SURE...

BUT IT'S MORE THAN JUST CRIMINAL INTUITION THAT I'M GOING ON HERE.

I DID MY RESEARCH, TOO.

SAME DAY THAT RICKY GOT SHOT, EIGHTY GRAND IN CASH WAS STOLEN FROM *TRAMWELL CONSTRUCTION.*

SOME *POLITICAL PAYOFF* OR SOMETHING, TAKEN FROM THEIR OFFICES AT GUNPOINT BY THREE MEN AND A WOMAN.

SO... OBVIOUSLY *SOMEONE* DIDN'T THINK THEIR CUT WAS BIG ENOUGH.

JESUS... KILLED OVER *EIGHTY GRAND*...

IT'S *PATHETIC*, YOU KNOW?

I ALWAYS... ONCE I GOT OLDER AND FOUND HOW FULL OF *SHIT* THEY ALL WERE... OUR PARENTS, I MEAN...

I ALWAYS THOUGHT YOU WERE *LUCKY* TO GET OUT... EVEN HOW YOU *DID*.

IN *BOSNIA*, TRACY HAD SEEN THINGS HE'D NEVER IMAGINED. THINGS HIS FATHER HADN'T SEEN IN VIETNAM, EVEN.

THINGS THAT DID, IN FACT, PHASE HIM.

AND HE HADN'T FELT LUCKY THEN. NOT AT ALL.

YOUR MAN *LEO* SAID TO SAY HEY.

YOU *SAW* HIM?

NAH. I DON'T GO TO NO PRISON *VOLUNTARILY,* NOT EVEN COUNTY LOCK-UP...

WE HAD A FRIEND IN THE *INFIRMARY* DOWN THERE GET IN TOUCH.

YOUR FRIEND'S STILL DOING THERAPY FROM HIS SURGERY A FEW MONTHS BACK.

YEAH, I *HEARD* HE TOOK A FEW BULLETS.

WAY I HEARD IT, THE MAN IS *LUCKY* TO BE ALIVE...

...'CEPT FOR BEING IN *JAIL.*

SO... IS THAT IT, THEN? DO I *QUALIFY?*

IF LEO PATTERSON -- WITH *HIS* REP -- SAYS YOU'RE A GOOD MAN TO WORK WITH...

...THAT'S ALL *I* NEED TO KNOW.

SO CAN WE ALL STOP BEING *VAGUE* NOW? WHAT EXACTLY *IS* THE JOB?

IT'S COMPLICATED.

THAT'S NOT *EXACTLY* WHAT I WAS HOPING TO HEAR

IT'S A TWO-PART JOB, THAT'S ALL.

AND WE GET *PAID* AFTER *PART TWO.*

YEAH, SEE... *THAT* DOESN'T SOUND RIGHT.

NORMALLY WE'D AGREE, BUT THERE'S NO MONEY *AT ALL* WITHOUT PART ONE.

I'LL ASK THE OBVIOUS QUESTION, THEN... WHAT'S *PART ONE?*

BREAKING OUR FRIEND OUT OF PRISON.

UH...

WHY?

'CAUSE THE PAYOUT IS *SIMON'S* SCORE. CAN'T TAKE IT DOWN WITHOUT HIM.

DON'T EVEN KNOW WHAT IT IS... 'CEPT IT'S *BIG.*

NELSON'S RIGHT, BUT WE ALSO KNOW WHEN IT HAS TO HAPPEN -- *CHRISTMAS EVE.*

WHICH GIVES US A *WEEK.*

OKAY... SO HOW DO WE GET TO THIS *SIMON?*

HE KINDA COMES TO *US*, ACTUALLY... SEE, SIMON'S OUT HERE AT *GRAZER STATE.*

HE'S GONNA FAKE A *HEART-ATTACK.* THEY CAN'T DEAL WITH ANYTHING THAT SERIOUS...

SO THEY POP HIM IN AN *AMBULANCE*, RACE TO THE CITY... AND WE GRAB HIM *HERE.*

CENTER CITY...? IN *BROAD DAYLIGHT?*

'CAUSE THERE'S ALMOST FIFTY MILES OF ROAD *BETWEEN* GRAZER AND THERE.

YOU EVER BEEN *OUT THERE?* IT'S *EMPTY.*

NOT EVEN A FUCKIN' *TUMBLEWEED* TO HIDE BEHIND.

COPS'D BE *ON US* IN NO TIME.

NO, CENTER CITY'S OUR SPOT...

YOU HAVE SOME *PROBLEM* WITH THAT?

NO...

JUST TRYING TO *MINIMIZE* OUR EXPOSURE.

TRACY HADN'T PLANNED TO SEE CENTER CITY AGAIN ANYTIME SOON... BUT THE PLAN WAS DECENT.

THOUGH HE FOUND ONE PART TO IMPROVE ON, THAT WOULD HOPEFULLY MAKE THE TRIP SMOOTHER, AND SHORTER

SIMON WAS APPARENTLY THE PLANNER IN THE CREW, WHAT THEY USED TO CALL A JUGGER OR JUGMARKER, IN THE OLD DAYS.

THE ONE WHO FOUND THE SCORES AND MAPPED OUT HOW TO TAKE THEM DOWN.

A FEW MONTHS AGO, HE'D BEEN CAUGHT DRIVING DRUNK AND HIS PAROLE WAS REVOKED.

BUT EVEN LOCKED AWAY IN PRISON, SIMON WAS STILL FIGURING ANGLES.

MEDIC!

LIKE WHICH MIXTURE OF *CRYSTAL METH* AND *VALIUM* WOULD MIMIC THE MOST BASIC SYMPTOMS OF A HEART-ATTACK.

JESUS... HIS *HEART-RATE'S* GOING CRAZY.

...MY ARM... FEELS *WRONG*...

WE GOTTA GET HIM TO AN E.R - *NOW.*

SO, TWO MORNINGS AFTER THEIR MEET AT THE HOTEL, TRACY AND THE OTHERS WERE WAITING NEAR THE FREEWAY OFFRAMP... READY.

SURE YOU KNOW WHAT YOU'RE DOIN'?

IF I MISS, YOU CAN ALWAYS TELL NELSON TO SWITCH TO *PLAN B* AND RAM THEM...

...BUT I *WON'T* MISS.

INCOMING BOYS, COMING RIGHT AT YOU.

I SEE IT.

PAK

PTTTT

DID YOU *HIT 'EM?*

SEE FOR YOURSELF, THEY'RE ALREADY PULLING OVER

WE GOTTA *MOVE.*

RIGHT. LET'S GO...

MAL - KEEP WATCH FOR THE PIGS AND FOLLOW OUR LEAD.

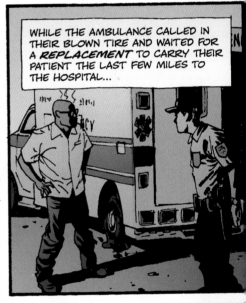

WHILE THE AMBULANCE CALLED IN THEIR BLOWN TIRE AND WAITED FOR A *REPLACEMENT* TO CARRY THEIR PATIENT THE LAST FEW MILES TO THE HOSPITAL...

...TRACY AND GRAY CIRCLED THE BLOCK IN A NEARLY IDENTICAL AMBULANCE STOLEN EARLIER THAT MORNING.

YOU *READY?*

I'M ONLY DRIVING FOR THIS PART... SO I'M *ALREADY* WORKING.

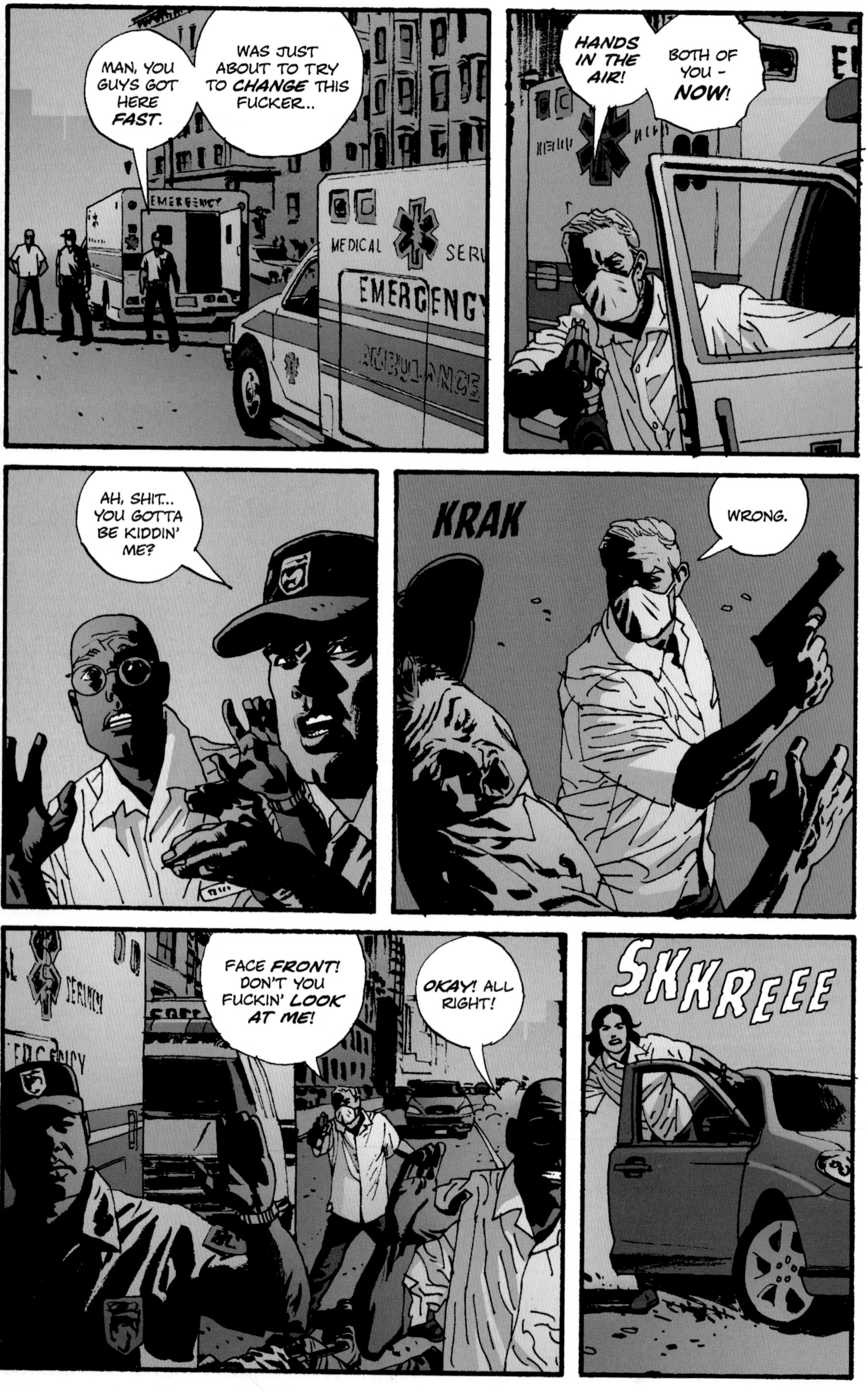
MAN, YOU GUYS GOT HERE FAST.
WAS JUST ABOUT TO TRY TO CHANGE THIS FUCKER..
EMERGENCY
MEDICAL SERV
EMERGENCY
AMBULANCE
HANDS IN THE AIR!
BOTH OF YOU - NOW!
AH, SHIT.. YOU GOTTA BE KIDDIN' ME?
KRAK
WRONG.
FACE FRONT! DON'T YOU FUCKIN' LOOK AT ME!
OKAY! ALL RIGHT!
SKKREEE

SET THE MAN *FREE*.

I'M ON IT.

SIMON? ARE YOU *OKAY*?

NOT MY FINEST... HOUR... SWEETIE.

HAVEN'T DONE... THAT MUCH DRUGS... SINCE THE *EIGHTIES*...

HENH... HEH...

OKAY... WE'RE JUST ABOUT THROUGH HERE.

NOW, DON'T ANY OF YOU *TURN AROUND* BEFORE WE LEAVE THE AREA, OKAY?

I DON'T WANNA HAVE TO SHOOT ANYBODY.

IT WENT OFF WITHOUT A HITCH.

NOW THEY SPLIT UP, GRAY AND NELSON TAKING SIMON IN THE *TOYOTA*, WHICH THE PARAMEDICS AND GUARDS HADN'T SEEN...

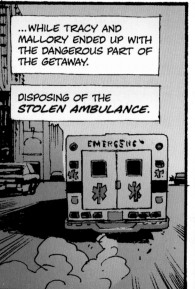

...WHILE TRACY AND MALLORY ENDED UP WITH THE DANGEROUS PART OF THE GETAWAY.

DISPOSING OF THE *STOLEN AMBULANCE.*

IT WOULD ONLY BE A MINUTE OR TWO BEFORE HALF THE COPS IN CENTER CITY WERE LOOKING FOR IT.

YOU WANNA HIT THOSE SIRENS AND *FLASHERS...* CLEAR US A PATH?

NAH... LET'S NOT DRAW ANY *MORE* ATTENTION THAN WE HAVE TO.

A COP JUST DROVE PAST BACK THERE.

YEAH, THE *OTHER* WAY... WE'RE GOOD.

TRUST ME. I KNOW HOW TO BLEND INTO THE BACKGROUND.

THAT WAS NICE WORK, TAKING OUT THEIR *TIRE*.

HOW LONG WERE YOU IN THE MILITARY?

LONG ENOUGH TO LEARN HOW TO SHOOT LIKE THAT.

I'M GUESSING A *LONG TIME*.

BUT I'M GUESSING IT NEVER *FIT* YOU, FOLLOWING ORDERS...

MALLORY WAS WRONG. AT FIRST, THE LIFE OF A SOLDIER HAD FIT HIM LIKE A SECOND SKIN.

HE'D FOUND A KIND OF FREEDOM WITHIN THE STRUCTURE.

THE LACK OF CHOICE WAS ACTUALLY A RELIEF.

NO ONE LIKES TO BE ORDERED AROUND.

ACTUALLY, SEEMS LIKE THAT'S WHAT *MOST* OF THE WORLD *DOES* LIKE...

LIKE ROBOTS... STOP ON RED, GO ON GREEN, PAY TAXES...

HELL, MOST OF THE IDIOTS PROBABLY EVEN *VOTE*.

CAN YOU *STOP* TALKING? I'M TRYING TO TORCH A VAN HERE...

OH, AM I RUINING YOUR BIG MOMENT?

YES.

FOR A MOMENT, WHEN SHE LAUGHED, HE KNEW WHAT RICK HAD SEEN IN HER

AND HE KNEW THAT WAS BAD... SHE WAS SUPPOSED TO BE HIS PATH TO THE TRUTH, NOTHING MORE.

LET'S GO... LONG DRIVE AHEAD.

ANYTHING ELSE WAS TROUBLE.

HEY, YEAH, THIS IS GUMBIE, AT THE JUNK-YARD...

YOU STILL LOOKIN' FOR A *MEAN-LOOKIN'* DUDE WITH A *BURN SCAR* ON HIS FACE ON ONE SIDE?

'CAUSE I THINK I JUST GOT HIS LICENSE PLATE FOR YA'...

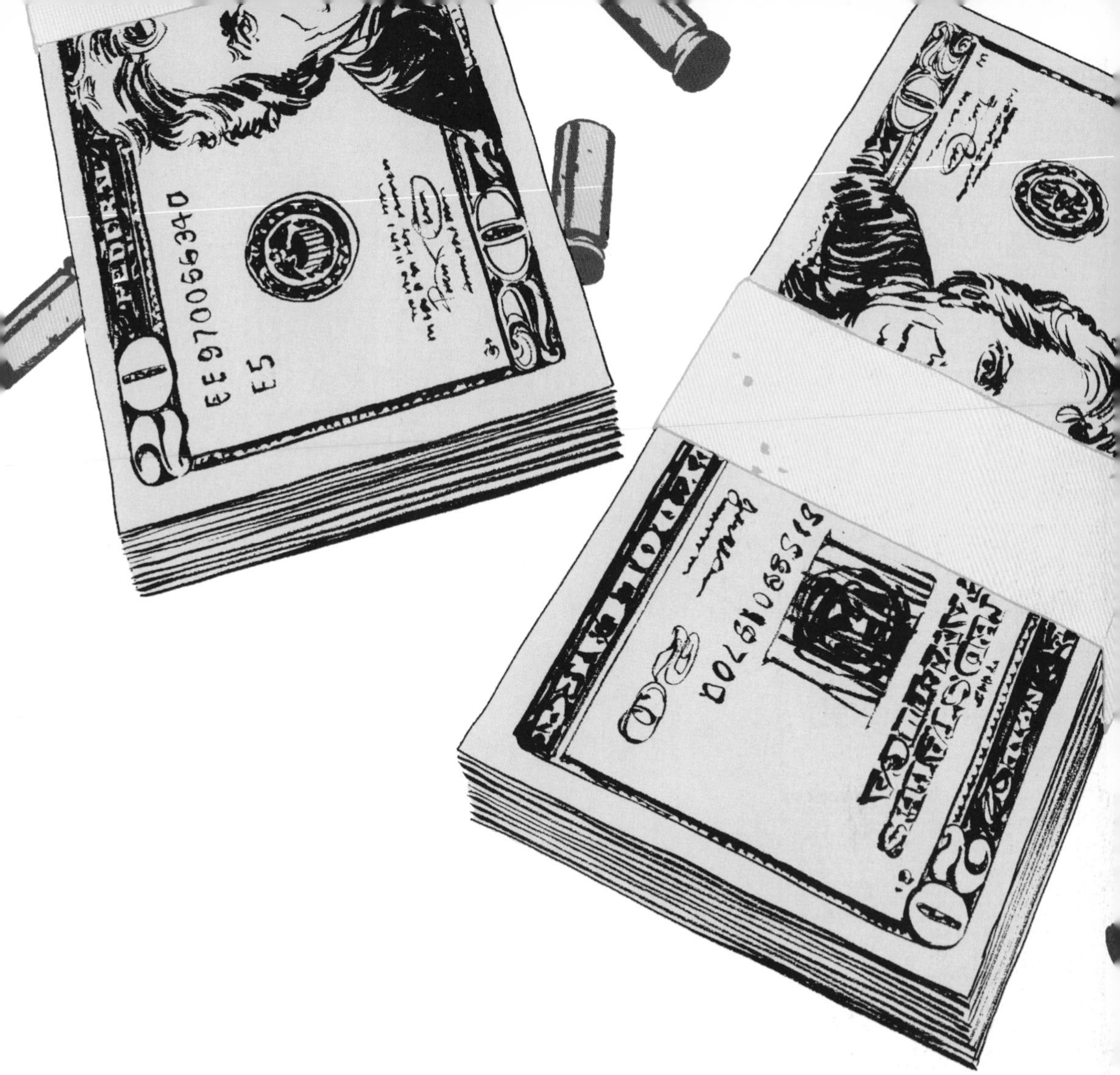

Part Three

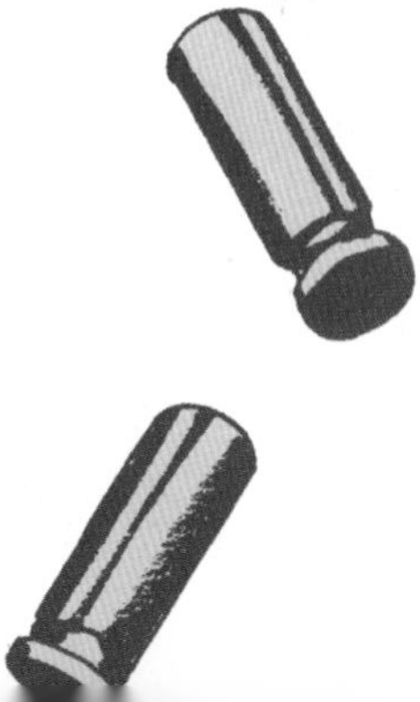

TRACY HADN'T SLEPT WELL SINCE HE WAS A LITTLE KID.

AND AS HE GOT OLDER, THE SCREAMING IN HIS HOME HAD BEEN REPLACED WITH THE SCREAMING OF WAR ZONES.

AT LEAST TWICE A WEEK, HE STILL WOKE THINKING OF THE WOMEN IN JARUGE. THEIR EYES LIKE AN ECHO THAT NEVER COMPLETELY FADED OUT...

...EVEN ON A NIGHT LIKE THIS.

WHAT ARE YOU DOING?

JUST WATCHING THE SNOW FALL...

I LIKE HOW IT MAKES THE CITY LOOK...

BEFORE ALL THE PEOPLE WAKE UP TO RUIN IT.

UNSPOILED.

YOU'RE A STRANGE GUY.

COME BACK TO BED AND I'LL SHOW YOU SPOILED, *SAM.*

SAM.

WHEN SHE SAYS IT, IT CUTS THROUGH HIM FOR A SECOND.

HE'S MAKING A MISTAKE HERE, AND HE KNOWS IT, BUT SOME THINGS YOU JUST CAN'T CONTROL...

...AND BESIDES, IT WASN'T LIKE HE'D HAD A PLAN FOR WHAT TO *DO* ONCE HE GOT IN WITH THESE PEOPLE.

LIQUOR

LIQUOR & WINE

1ST NATIONAL TRUST

HE WAS JUST MAKING IT UP AS HE WENT ALONG...

ANY CHANCE YOU'LL TELL ME WHAT EXACTLY WE'RE WAITING FOR?

YOU'LL SEE. PATIENCE IS A VIRTUE.

I'M PRETTY SURE IGNORANCE *ISN'T*, THOUGH.

OKAY, OKAY... I'LL GIVE YOU A HINT.

I'M WAITING FOR THAT OLD MAN TO LOCK UP HIS LIQUOR STORE AND GO HOME.

CLOSED

BECAUSE I'D RATHER NOT HAVE ANY WITNESSES STANDING AROUND.

WITNESSES TO *WHAT*?

BANK ROBBERY. *DUH.*

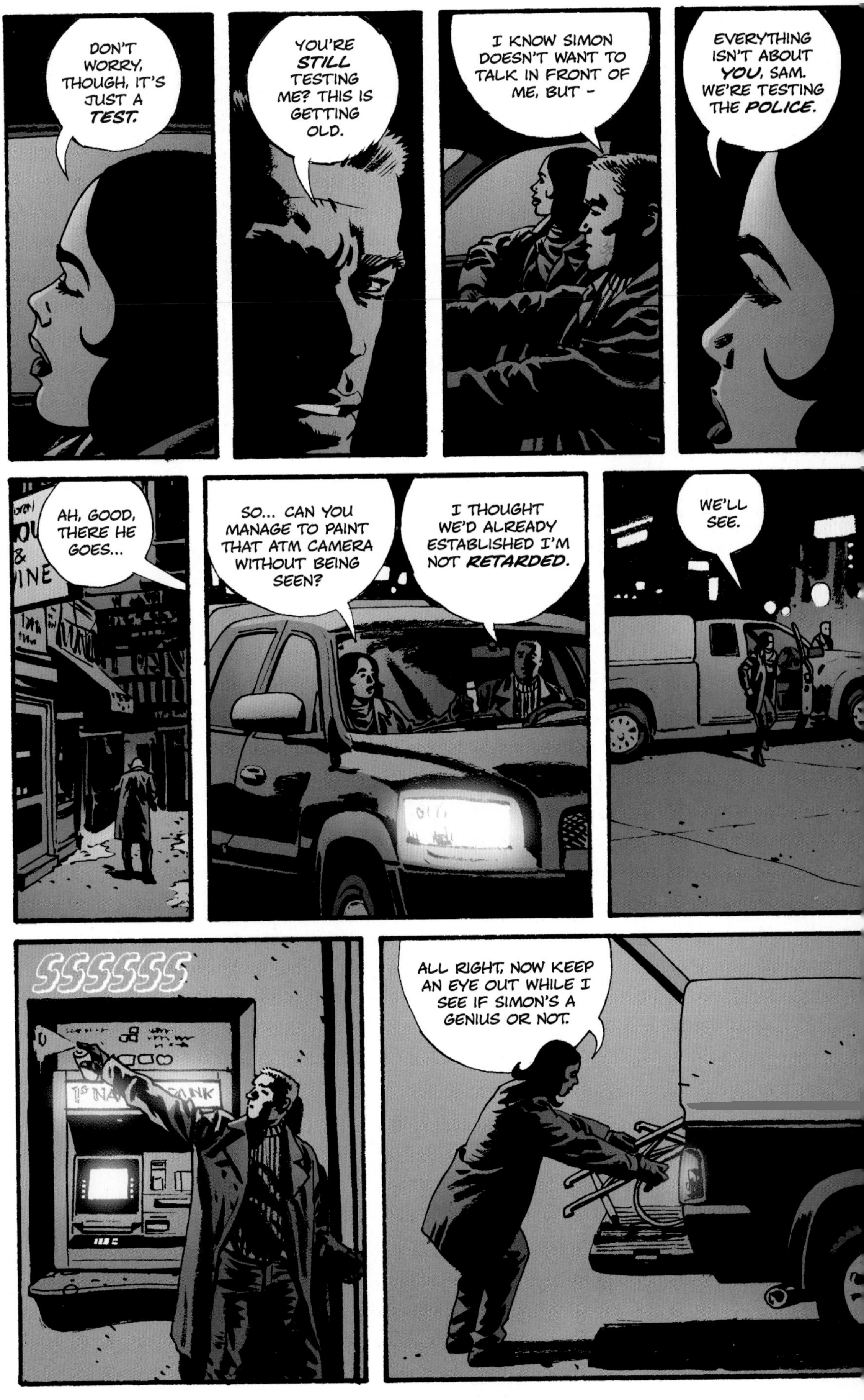
DON'T WORRY, THOUGH, IT'S JUST A *TEST.*
YOU'RE *STILL* TESTING ME? THIS IS GETTING OLD.
I KNOW SIMON DOESN'T WANT TO TALK IN FRONT OF ME, BUT -
EVERYTHING ISN'T ABOUT *YOU*, SAM. WE'RE TESTING THE *POLICE*.
AH, GOOD, THERE HE GOES...
SO... CAN YOU MANAGE TO PAINT THAT ATM CAMERA WITHOUT BEING SEEN?
I THOUGHT WE'D ALREADY ESTABLISHED I'M NOT *RETARDED*.
WE'LL SEE.
SSSSSS
ALL RIGHT, NOW KEEP AN EYE OUT WHILE I SEE IF SIMON'S A GENIUS OR NOT.

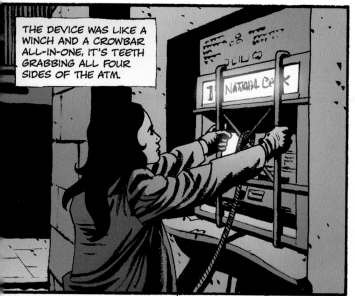
THE DEVICE WAS LIKE A WINCH AND A CROWBAR ALL-IN-ONE, IT'S TEETH GRABBING ALL FOUR SIDES OF THE ATM.

THE TRUCK WOULD PROVIDE THE REST OF THE LEVERAGE.

SIMON SAID IT SHOULD BE LIKE POPPING THE LID OFF A CAN.

OKAY, FLOOR IT.

VRROOOOM

SSQQWEEEE

KRAAAK

HA! AWESOME!

LANGALANGALANGALANGALANGLANGALANGALANGA

DID YOU SERIOUSLY JUST SAY *AWESOME*?

SHUT UP AND HELP ME GET THIS SHIT...

LANGALANGALANGALANGALANGLANGALANGALANGA

I CAN SAY AWESOME.

ALL RIGHT, WHERE WE GOING?

LANGALANGALANGALANGALANGLANGALANGALANGA

THAT PARKING GARAGE, TOP LEVEL.

LANGALANGA

WELL... THAT WAS A BUZZ

LANGALANGALANGALANGALANGLANGA

YEAH... AWESOME.

OH, SHUT UP, MISTER I-NEVER-SMILE.

YOU'RE JUST JEALOUS THAT I ENJOY MY WORK.

WHEEOOOOO WHEEEOOOOO

WHAT DO YOU HAVE? FEELS LIKE FIVE MINUTES.

ALMOST SIX, SINCE THE ALARM WENT OFF.

THESE COPS ARE SOFT AS PLAY-DOUGH.

SO, NOW WE WAIT AROUND FOR THEM TO WRAP IT UP? COULD BE HOURS.

YEAH, BUT IT'D DRAW TOO MUCH ATTENTION TO JUST DRIVE OFF NOW.

THERE'S A BAR DOWN THE STREET... WE'LL COME BACK.

IT WAS A YUPPIE BAR THAT WAS MOSTLY EMPTY, EXCEPT FOR A FEW COKED-UP BUSINESSMEN AND THEIR HIGH-END CALL-GIRLS.

MALLORY AND TRACY WERE OUT OF PLACE THERE, BUT IT WAS LATE, SO NO ONE NOTICED.

AND AFTER A FEW DRINKS, THEIR KIDDING AROUND HAD MOVING ON TO SERIOUS FLIRTING.

IT HAD BEEN A LONG TIME SINCE A WOMAN HAD LOOKED AT HIM LIKE THAT...

YOU SURE YOU AREN'T JUST *DRUNK* HERE, MAL?

NOT *JUST*... NO. I KNOW WHAT I'M DOING.

I DON'T WANNA MESS UP OUR WORK.

ME EITHER... BUT WHAT GOOD IS THIS LIFE IF YOU CAN'T LET YOUR *HAIR DOWN* SOMETIMES?

BESIDES... IT DOESN'T HAVE TO *MEAN ANYTHING*...

WHICH WAS EXACTLY THE LIE HE NEEDED TO HEAR

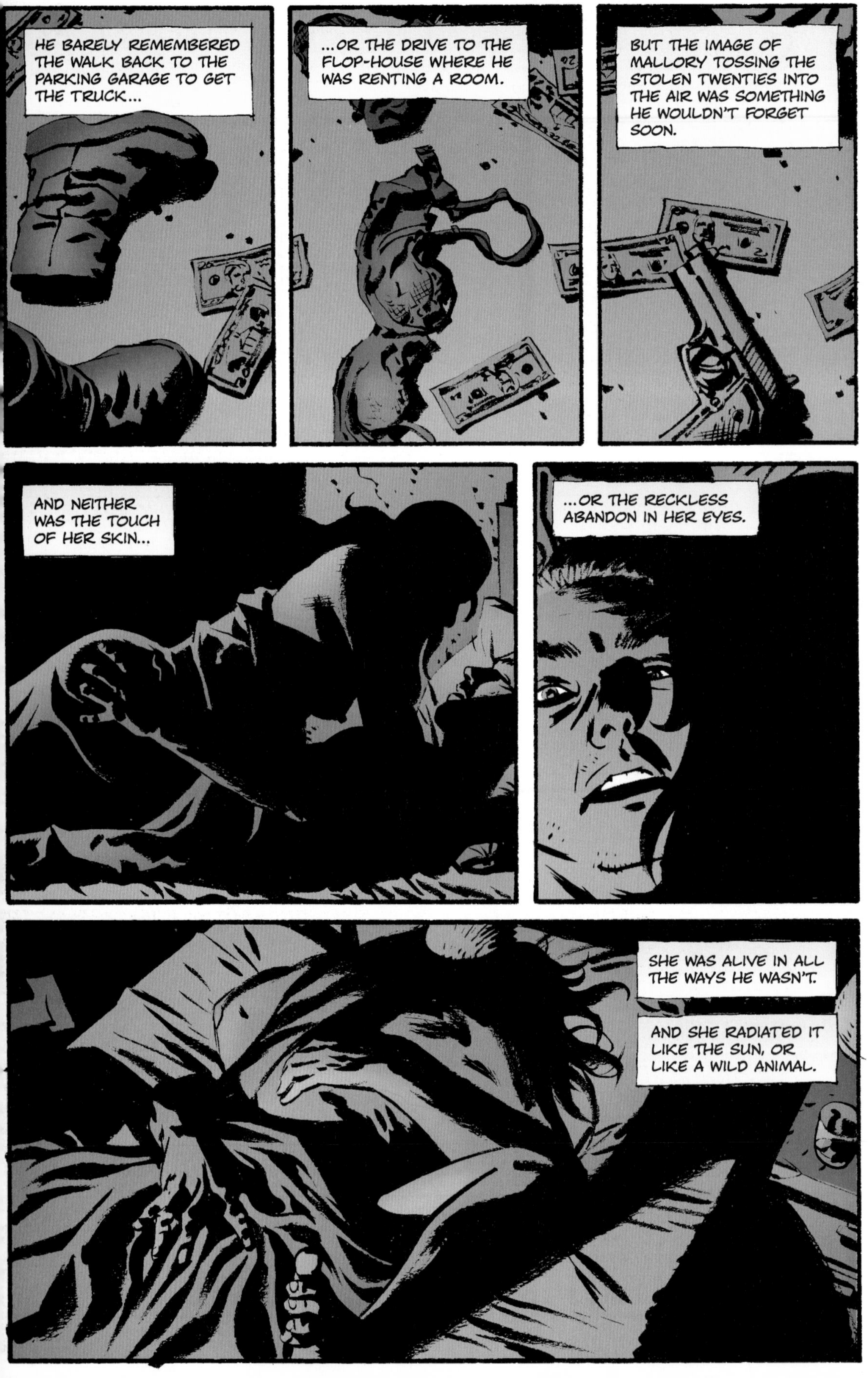
HE BARELY REMEMBERED THE WALK BACK TO THE PARKING GARAGE TO GET THE TRUCK...
...OR THE DRIVE TO THE FLOP-HOUSE WHERE HE WAS RENTING A ROOM.
BUT THE IMAGE OF MALLORY TOSSING THE STOLEN TWENTIES INTO THE AIR WAS SOMETHING HE WOULDN'T FORGET SOON.
AND NEITHER WAS THE TOUCH OF HER SKIN...
...OR THE RECKLESS ABANDON IN HER EYES.
SHE WAS ALIVE IN ALL THE WAYS HE WASN'T.
AND SHE RADIATED IT LIKE THE SUN, OR LIKE A WILD ANIMAL.

LATER, HE WATCHED HER SLEEP AND THOUGHT ABOUT HIS LITTLE BROTHER.

WAS THIS SOME KIND OF BETRAYAL? IT FELT LIKE IT MUST BE. BUT HE'D BETRAYED RICKY SO MANY TIMES BEFORE.

THE SAD TRUTH WAS, ALTHOUGH HE LOVED HIS BROTHER IN WAYS HE COULD NEVER EXPRESS...

...HE HAD NEVER REALLY LIKED HIM THAT MUCH WHEN THEY WERE KIDS.

HE REMEMBERED ALL THE TIMES HE GAVE HIM INDIAN BURNS, OR DITCHED HIM.

RICKY WAS A TAGALONG, AND SOMEONE WHO NEEDED TO BE LOOKED AFTER A HASSLE.

IT HURT REMEMBERING HOW MANY TIMES HE'D MADE THE KID CRY... AND LAUGHED ABOUT IT, EVEN.

HAD MALLORY BROUGHT HIS BROTHER SOME KIND OF PEACE? OR HAPPINESS?

HE HOPED SO.

AND HE HOPED HE WOULDN'T HAVE TO KILL HER.

THE REST OF THE CREW, THOUGH, HE COULD GO EITHER WAY ON...

ARE YOU *SERIOUSLY* CHECKING ME FOR A *WIRE*?

GONE OUT O BUSINE

SORRY, MAN... *SIMON'S* IN CHARGE NOW, NEW RULES.

NOTHING PERSONAL. I JUST DON'T *KNOW YOU*, NEW GUY.

HELL, I ONLY *BARELY* TRUSTED THE GUY YOU'RE REPLACING.

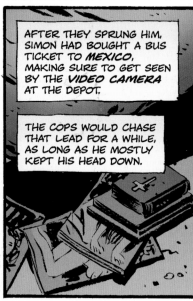

AFTER THEY SPRUNG HIM, SIMON HAD BOUGHT A BUS TICKET TO *MEXICO*, MAKING SURE TO GET SEEN BY THE *VIDEO CAMERA* AT THE DEPOT.

THE COPS WOULD CHASE THAT LEAD FOR A WHILE, AS LONG AS HE MOSTLY KEPT HIS HEAD DOWN.

I GOT YOU OUT OF *PRISON*, OLD MAN.

THAT'S THE *ONLY REASON* YOU'RE STILL AROUND AT ALL.

BUT DON'T THINK 'CAUSE MALLORY SPREADS HER LEGS FOR YOU, THE *REST OF US* ARE PLANNING TO BEND OVER

MAL'S GOT HER *PROBLEMS*, YOU'RE JUST ANOTHER ONE OF THEM NOW.

WHAT THE HELL DOES *THAT* MEAN?

THINK YOU'RE THE ONLY GUY IN THIS CREW SHE'S FUCKED?

JUST *DON'T* LET IT AFFECT THE JOB.

SHE WON'T.

YOU REALLY **DON'T** WANNA POINT THAT **FINGER** AT ME, GRAY.

HE'LL POINT WHATEVER HE **WANTS** AT YOU, AND SO WILL I...

SEE?

EASY, NELSON... ALL OF YOU...

LET'S NOT GET UGLY.

WE'RE JUST TRYING TO MAKE SURE YOU UNDERSTAND THE **HIERARCHY** HERE, SAM.

I THINK I GET THE PICTURE.

BUT NO ONE'S BEGRUDGING YOU WANTING SOME **GASH** IN YOUR DIET.

HELL, IT'S **ALL** I BEEN EATIN' THE LAST FEW DAYS, AN' MY TASTES RUN **WEIRDER** THAN YOURS.

CAN WE GET BACK TO **BUSINESS** NOW?

SURE, KID... LET'S DO THAT.

WHAT? AM I LATE?

THOUGHT YOU GUYS SAID **FIVE?**

THAT'S OKAY, SWEETIE... YOU DIDN'T MISS ANYTHING.

I WAS JUST ABOUT TO DO THE **RUNDOWN** ON THE SCORE...

SAM! WAIT UP A MINUTE!

WAS HE *REALLY* ANGRY? HE DIDN'T KNOW THE ANSWER TO THAT...

...BUT *PRETENDING* TO BE MIGHT HELP HIM GET TO *OTHER* ANSWERS.

WHAT? WHAT DID THEY SAY BEFORE I GOT THERE?

DON'T WORRY ABOUT IT.

THEY JUST KNEW ABOUT US. TOLD ME NOT TO FEEL SPECIAL.

THOSE *FUCKHEADS.*

DON'T LISTEN TO THEM.

I DON'T, BUT I DON'T KNOW *YOU* MUCH BETTER THAN I KNOW THEM.

LISTEN. THE ONLY MAN IN THAT ROOM I EVER *TOUCHED* IS YOU.

OKAY. THEN WHAT ARE THEY *TALKING* ABOUT?

JUST... ANCIENT HISTORY.

GUESS YOU REMIND THEM OF SOMEONE A LITTLE.

WHO'S *THAT?*

IT DOESN'T MATTER DON'T EVEN *LOOK* LIKE HIM. JUST... SOMETHING ABOUT YOU...

IT MATTERS TO *ME*. THEY PUT A GUN TO MY HEAD.

WHAT?

CHRIST... I *DID* MISS A LOT.

AND I'M STILL IN THE DARK HERE, MALLORY.

I SAID IT DOESN'T MATTER AND IT *DOESN'T*.

SO I LIKE TO GET *LAID* AFTER A JOB SOMETIMES.

HAVE A LITTLE *FUN* AFTER THE *TENSION* BREAKS.

IF THEY CAN'T HANDLE THAT, OR IF *YOU* CAN'T...

...THEN YOU CAN ALL GO FUCK YOURSELVES.

DID YOU HEAR *ME* COMPLAINING ABOUT *YOU?*

I JUST WANNA *KNOW* WHAT I'M GETTING INTO.

AND HERE I THOUGHT YOU ALREADY KNEW...

HE REMINDED THEM OF HIS BROTHER? HE WASN'T EXPECTING THAT.

THE TWO OF THEM COULDN'T HAVE *BEEN* MORE DIFFERENT UP TO THE DAY THAT TRACY LEFT.

LEO SAID RICKY HAD CHANGED, BUT JUST *WHAT* HAD HE CHANGED INTO?

THIS HAD TO *HURT*...

WHAT? OH... *THAT.* NOT SO MUCH.

NOT AT FIRST.

IT'S NOT THAT *OLD*, IS IT? WHAT HAPPENED?

WHAT DO YOU *THINK* HAPPENED?

I GOT BURNED.

...WHAT... YOU DOING...?

JUST GOING TO GET COFFEE AND STUFF.

SLEEP. I LIKE YOU THAT WAY...

INSTEAD OF HIS USUAL NIGHTMARES, HE WOKE THAT MORNING THINKING ABOUT HIS FATHER.

DID HE REMIND MALLORY OF RICKY BECAUSE THEY HAD *BOTH* ENDED UP LIKE THEIR DAD, SOMEHOW?

AFTER ALL THE YEARS HE'D TRIED TO BE ANYTHING *BUT* HIS FATHER, WAS THERE SOME PIECE OF THAT BASTARD IN HIM ANYWAY?

THAT'S WHAT HE WAS THINKING ABOUT WHEN HE ALMOST DIED.

SHIT...

KKSSSH!

UTT—

THERE WERE TWO MORE ACROSS THE STREET. WHERE THE FUCK DID THESE GUYS COME FROM?

AS IT TURNED OUT, THESE GUYS HAD BEEN LOOKING FOR HIM FOR THREE DAYS, EVER SINCE HE AND THE OTHERS HAD SPRUNG SIMON IN CENTER CITY.

HIS CAR HAD BEEN TRACED BACK TO THE DEALER, WHO TOLD THEM EVERYTHING HE KNEW.

--NAME'S *SAM WEST.* GOT A COPY OF HIS LICENSE HERE SOMEWHERE...

LET ME GUESS, HE PAID *CASH?*

UH...

HAND IT OVER

AW, COME ON.

I'LL BREAK YOUR KNEECAPS AN' TAKE IT ANYWAY.

DAMN IT... KNEW THAT ASSHOLE WAS *TROUBLE.*

MORE THAN YOU *KNOW,* MAN.

LUCKY YOU DIDN'T TRY TO *SPEND* ANY OF THIS...

AND AFTER SOME LEGWORK, THE I.D. HAD LED TO THE FLEABAG HE WAS STAYING IN.

BUT TRACY DIDN'T KNOW ANY OF THIS.

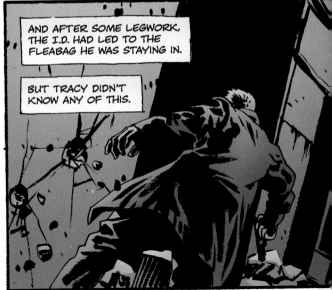

HE JUST KNEW THEY WERE TRYING TO KILL HIM.

BUT THE SNOW WOULD SLOW THEM DOWN...

...AND THEIR *SILENCERS* MEANT THEY HAD TO GET IN CLOSE.

SO HE'D USE THAT.

GERRY!

AHHH!

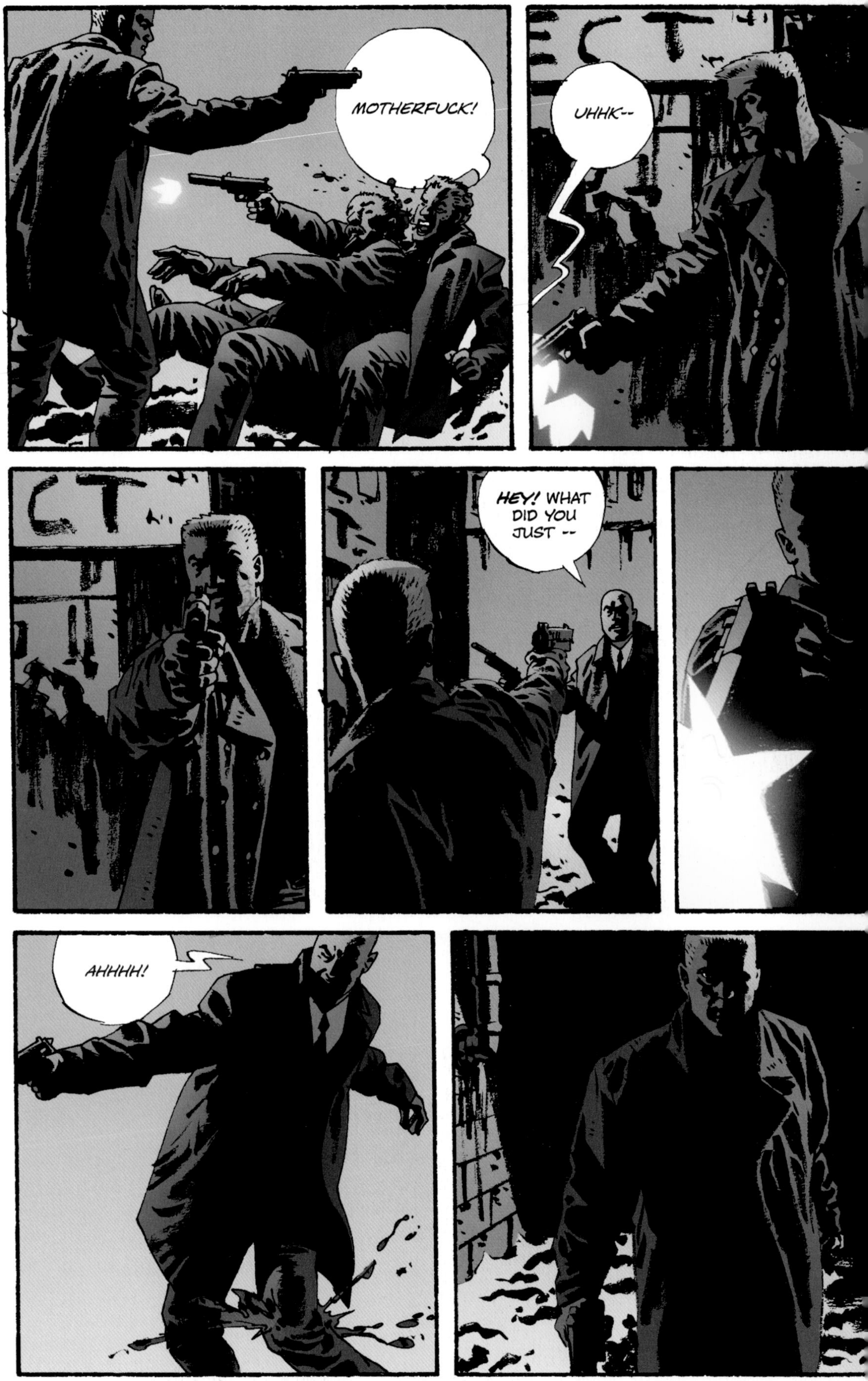
MOTHERFUCK!
UHHK--
HEY! WHAT DID YOU JUST --
AHHHH!

WHY ARE YOU AFTER ME?

...SCREW YOU... FUCKIN' BASTARD...

WRONG.

YYAAAAIIIIEEEE!

ONE MORE TRY.

DON'T - DON'T... PLEASE...

I DON'T... GERRY KNEW...

ALL I KNOW IS... S'POSED TO TAKE CARE OF YOU.

THEN WHO DO YOU WORK FOR?

GERRY... I WORK FOR GERRY.

SHIT.

THAT MANY SHOTS FIRED, SOMEONE HAD TO HAVE CALLED THE COPS BY NOW.

STILL, HE KNEW THE CITY, AND KNEW NO ONE EVER *SAW* ANYTHING ON THESE STREETS.

HE JUST HAD TO GET OUT OF THERE, AND FAST.

SOMEONE KNEW *WHERE* HE WAS, AT LEAST... IF NOT *WHO*.

THAT WAS QUICK... BARELY HAD TIME TO TAKE A SHOWER

WHERE'S THE COFFEE?

OH, *YEAH*... I WAS THINKING...

...LET'S GO *OUT* FOR BREAKFAST INSTEAD.

MISTER HYDE... *SEBASTIAN?*

YOU GOT THE *REPORT*, ABOUT GERRY AND HIS TEAM?

YES. AND I WAS UNDER THE *IMPRESSION* THAT GERRY WAS GOOD AT HIS JOB.

HE WAS.

THEN WHO THE HELL *IS* THIS SAM WEST PERSON?

HOW DOES HE KILL *FOUR* TRAINED MEN AND JUST *WALK AWAY?*

I DON'T KNOW, SIR.

SHIT... I'LL BET THE SON OF A BITCH DOESN'T EVEN KNOW WHAT HE *STOLE.*

"WELL, ONLY A *BANK* WOULD BE ABLE TO TELL."

HAPPY HOLIDAY

COUNTERFEIT?

OH, YOU HAVE *GOT* TO BE KIDDING ME?!

Part Four

THE ONLY PERSON THAT TRACY WAS EVER AFRAID OF WAS HIS FATHER.

HIS EARLIEST MEMORIES WERE VAGUE, HAZY IMAGES AT BEST... BUT HE REMEMBERED SCREAMING.

HE REMEMBERED HIS FATHER'S VOICE, YELLING.

AND HE REMEMBERED FEAR.

A FEAR SO TOTAL THAT HE WAS WRAPPED IN IT.

IN HIS LIFE, NO ONE SCARED HIM. NO ONE MADE HIM FLINCH.

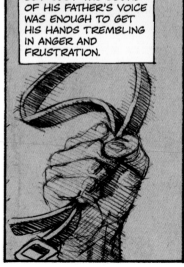

BUT JUST THE SOUND OF HIS FATHER'S VOICE WAS ENOUGH TO GET HIS HANDS TREMBLING IN ANGER AND FRUSTRATION.

AND HE HATED HIMSELF FOR THAT.

UNLIKE MOST BOYS, INCLUDING HIS BROTHER, HE DIDN'T CRAVE ACCEPTANCE OR ADMIRATION FROM HIS DAD.

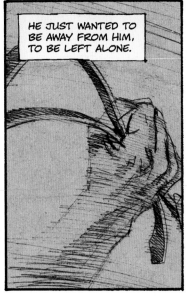

HE JUST WANTED TO BE AWAY FROM HIM, TO BE LEFT ALONE.

RICKY WAS THE OTHER WAY, THOUGH.

HE WASN'T AFRAID OF THEIR FATHER AT ALL, HE WAS JUST AFRAID OF LETTING HIM DOWN.

AND DESPITE THE BEATINGS AND THE BOOZE AND THE WOMEN AND EVERYTHING...

...HE LOVED HIM THE WAY A SON IS SUPPOSED TO... WITH AWE.

RICKY, EVEN AS A LITTLE KID, WAS PROUD TO BE A LAWLESS.

PROUD TO HAVE A FAMOUS FATHER, EVEN IF HE WAS FAMOUS FOR BEING A MONSTER.

TO TRACY, THOUGH, THEIR NAME HAD ALWAYS BEEN A BURDEN.

HE'D SPENT HALF HIS CHILDHOOD WISHING HE COULD BE SOMEONE ELSE...

WILL PLAY SANTA FOR FOOD

...BUT NOW *THAT* WAS BECOMING A PROBLEM, TOO.

COME ON, YOU LAZY BASTARD... PICK UP THE PHONE...

HELLO?

JAKE, IT'S *ME.* LISTEN, I NEED A FAVOR...

YOU *FUCKING ASSHOLE.*

I SPENT HALF A DAY FILLING OUT A *POLICE REPORT* BECAUSE OF YOU.

WHAT? WHAT THE FUCK ARE YOU TALKING ABOUT?

TRIED TO *DEPOSIT* SOME OF THE MONEY YOU GAVE ME, AND GUESS WHAT?

IT'S FUCKING *COUNTERFEIT!*

SHIT...

WAIT, WHEN WAS THIS?

YOU DIDN'T *TELL THEM* ABOUT ME, DID YOU?

IT WAS *TODAY,* ASSHOLE... AND NO, I DIDN'T *TELL THEM* ABOUT YOU.

SAID I FOUND IT IN THE *GUTTER,* DOWNTOWN.

I DON'T GENERALLY LIKE TO *ADMIT* TO TAKING PART IN *CRIMINAL ENTERPRISES.*

JACOB... RELAX... JUST RELAX...

I'M RELAXED, TRACY. BUT I WANT MY MONEY.

LOOK, WAIT A FEW DAYS AND I'LL *DOUBLE* WHAT I PAID BEFORE, OKAY?

SO YOU GOT ALL THE WAY *IN* WITH RICK'S OLD CREW, HUNH?

YEAH, FOR *NOW*... BUT THINGS ARE GETTING DICEY...

HAD SOME *PROFESSIONALS* AFTER ME THIS MORNING, AND I NEED HELP FIGURING OUT WHERE THEY *CAME FROM*.

AND WHY THEY'RE AFTER *ME*.

NO. I TOLD YOU, THAT'S *NOT* MY WORLD.

YOU *ALREADY* GOT ME FURTHER BACK INTO IT THAN I *SHOULD'VE*.

YOU WANT ANSWERS ABOUT YOUR BULLSHIT, ASK SOMEONE AT THE *UNDERTOW*.

JAKE, DON'T BE A DICK.

CALL ME WHEN YOU'VE GOT MY MONEY — *clik!*

DAMN IT.

SO THE MONEY HE'D STOLEN IN *CENTER CITY* WAS COUNTERFEIT.

THAT WAS *INTERESTING*, BUT DID IT EXPLAIN THE MEN WAITING FOR HIM THIS MORNING?

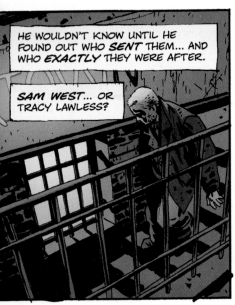

HE WOULDN'T KNOW UNTIL HE FOUND OUT WHO **SENT** THEM.... AND WHO **EXACTLY** THEY WERE AFTER.

SAM WEST... OR TRACY LAWLESS?

HE'D DONE A LOT OF BAD THINGS IN THE PAST FEW WEEKS, AND TOLD A LOT OF LIES TO BAD PEOPLE.

ANY OF THAT COULD BE BLOWING BACK AT HIM NOW.

SORRY ABOUT PULLIN' MY PIECE ON YOU LAST NIGHT.

THAT LOOK IN YOUR EYE, THOUGH YOU WAS ABOUT TO **KILL** GREY.

DON'T SWEAT IT, NELSON...

YOU GUYS ARE A **TIGHT** CREW, I UNDERSTAND...

ME BEING THE NEWCOMER, AN' ALL.

GLAD TO HEAR IT.

DON'T BE NEEDIN' NO BULLSHIT BETWEEN US TOMORROW NIGHT...

SO, YOU THREE'VE BEEN TOGETHER A LONG TIME, HUNH?

SORTA.

USED TO BE A FEW OTHERS, TOO...

LEO SAID SOME OLD FRIEND OF HIS USED TO RUN THIS CREW...

I CAN'T PICTURE GREY TAKIN' *ORDERS*, THOUGH.

SHIT, RICKY NEVER RAN *SHIT*.

ALWAYS BEEN SIMON'S *PLANS*... AN' US DOIN' THE REAL WORK.

I GUESS I HEARD WRONG...

NAH... RICKY LAWLESS *WAS* A HEAVY-HITTER.

BUT WE DON'T *TALK* ABOUT HIM NO MORE.

WHY NOT?

'CAUSE SOME SHIT'S BETTER LEFT *UNSAID*, Y'KNOW?

ANYWAY, THAT WASN'T EVEN *ABOUT* ME... I STAYED OUTTA THAT SHIT.

JUST DO WHAT I'M TOLD AND GET PAID.

BE BACK IN A MINUTE...

DON'T DRINK MY WHISKEY OR I *WILL* SHOOT YOU.

NOT A PROBLEM.

AT FIRST TRACY HAD FELT STRANGE COMING INTO THE UNDERTOW.

LIKE HE WAS STEPPING INTO SOMEONE ELSE'S SKIN... HIS BROTHER'S, OR HIS FATHER'S.

BUT WITHOUT HIM EVEN NOTICING, THAT HAD FADED.

GET ANOTHER PINT OF GUINNESS?

SURE, YOU CAN...

...TRACY.

EXCUSE ME?

YEAH, I RECOGNIZE YOU.

NOT THAT YOU LOOK MUCH LIKE THE KID I REMEMBER.

GNARLY, WHO'VE YOU TOLD?

THINK I'D BE IN BUSINESS IF I TALKED TO PEOPLE ABOUT PEOPLE?

I'M NEUTRAL, KID... I'M SWITZERLAND.

TO BE HONEST, I DIDN'T REALLY KNOW UNTIL THE OTHER DAY...

JUST KNEW YOU WERE FAMILIAR.

THEN SOME **HARDCASES** CAME IN ASKING ABOUT A GUY WITH A SCAR...

GUY NAMED **SAM**.

SHIT.

THAT CLINCHED IT. MEN WITH GUNS COMING INTO **MY** BAR... LOOKING FOR **YOU**.

KNEW YOU HAD TO BE A LAWLESS.

YOU KNOW WHO THESE GUYS WERE **WORKING** FOR?

NO, AND I DON'T **WANNA** KNOW, EITHER.

I'M TALKING TO YOU FOR **ONE REASON**... MALLORY.

I DON'T KNOW **WHAT** YOU'RE UP TO, BUT I KNOW IT AIN'T **GOOD**.

AN' IF ANYTHING **HAPPENS** TO THAT GIRL...

...NOT EVEN THE ARMY'LL BE ABLE TO SAVE YOU **THIS TIME**. UNDERSTAND ME?

JESUS... YOU **REALLY** DON'T REMEMBER ME...

OH, I **DO**, TRACY... BUT DON'T KID YOURSELF.

YOU'VE GOT THOSE **SAME** COLD EYES YOUR DADDY HAD...

YOU'RE A **LAWLESS**, AND IN THE END...

...YOU'RE ALL THE SAME.

SO... WHAT DO YOU *THINK*?

SORRY... WHAT?

OH, C'MON... DON'T TELL ME THIS DOESN'T DO *ANYTHING* FOR YOU.

YOU HAVE TO HAVE AT LEAST *ONE* NUN FANTASY...

I DON'T KNOW... I MEAN, YOU WEAR IT WELL...

...BUT I DIDN'T GO TO *CATHOLIC SCHOOL*.

GUESS I DON'T HAVE THOSE KIND OF ISSUES.

WHAT'S *UP* WITH YOU? YOU'VE BEEN *DISTRACTED* ALL NIGHT.

AND WHY'D YOU MOVE FROM ONE SHITHOLE HOTEL TO *ANOTHER*?

JUST PLAYIN' IT SAFE, SO CLOSE TO *THE JOB* AND ALL.

HE'D TAKEN HIS FEW BELONGINGS WITH HIM THAT MORNING WHEN HE AND MALLORY WENT TO BREAKFAST...

THEN HE'D FOUND A PLACE WITH A CLERK SO DRUNK HE WOULDN'T REMEMBER *WHO* CHECKED IN OR OUT, *OR* WHAT THEY LOOKED LIKE.

THE WALKWRIGHT INN

HE STASHED HIS CAR IN AN UNDERGROUND *PAY LOT.*

HE WOULDN'T NEED IT UNTIL THE NEXT DAY, ANYWAY.

IS THAT *IT*, YOU JUST TENSE BEFORE THE JOB?

NOT EXACTLY...

THEN *WHAT?*

NELSON SAID SOMETHING TONIGHT...

...IMPLIED SOME BAD SHIT WENT DOWN IN YOUR CREW A WHILE BACK.

NELSON TALKS TOO MUCH WHEN HE DRINKS.

HE DIDN'T *SAY* MUCH...I WAS READING BETWEEN THE LINES.

AND WHAT DID YOU FIND THERE?

THAT SOMEONE GOT KILLED.

SOMEONE NAMED RICKY.

THAT THERE WAS SOME KINDA RIFT BETWEEN HIM AND SIMON OVER SOMETHING.

SOME KIND OF *RIFT*... THAT'S A FUNNY WAY TO PUT IT.

SO, WHAT *HAPPENED*, THEN?

NOTHING THAT CONCERNS YOU... REALLY.

IF SIMON'S PUTTING BULLETS IN PARTNERS, *THAT* CONCERNS ME.

A LOT.

THAT ISN'T... LOOK, YOU KNOW THIS LIFE.

PARTNERS SQUABBLE, JOBS GO WRONG, PEOPLE SOMETIMES END UP DEAD...

BUT YOU DON'T NEED TO WORRY... NOT ABOUT *SIMON*, THAT'S FOR SURE.

WE WON'T EVEN *SEE HIM* AGAIN UNTIL AFTER THE SCORE.

SO CAN WE *PLEASE* CHANGE THE SUBJECT?

LIKE... WHY DON'T YOU GUESS IF I'M WEARING ANYTHING *UNDER* THIS?

OKAY... SURE...

CAREFUL THOUGH... ANSWER WRONG AND SISTER MALLORY FROM *OUR LADY OF MULTIPLE ORGASMS* WILL BE DEALING OUT *DISCIPLINE.*

LATER, IN THE MIDDLE OF THE NIGHT, MALLORY WAKES ALONE.

SHE KNOWS HE HAS TROUBLE SLEEPING. THAT HE HAS TERRIBLE NIGHTMARES.

SHE FIGURES HE'S PROBABLY OUT WALKING. OUT IN THE COLD AND THE SNOW.

BUT SHE'S NOT SEARCHING HIS ROOM, SHE TELLS HERSELF.

SHE'S JUST LOOKING FOR A LIGHTER...

FUCK...?

SHE'D NEVER SEEN IT BEFORE, OR... SHE DIDN'T THINK SHE HAD.

BUT SOMETHING ABOUT IT SEEMED FAMILIAR...

On the gravestones:

Angela
Lawless
[19]45-1979
Beloved

TEEGAR
LAWLESS
1942-1989

BRODERI[CK]
LAWLES[S]
1972-200[?]
REST IN PEA[CE]

HE HADN'T BEEN TO THE GRAVEYARD SINCE HIS MOTHER'S FUNERAL.

MOST OF THE YEAR BEFORE HER DEATH, TEEG HAD BEEN ON THE *RUN* AND HAD DRAGGED TRACY ALONG WITH HIM.

OKAY... HOLD IT STEADY... DON'T SPEED HERE.

BECAUSE A MAN AND A BOY TRAVELING TOGETHER ARE LESS SUSPICIOUS TO THE AUTHORITIES...

...AND BECAUSE HE NEEDED A GETAWAY DRIVER.

GO! GO! FLOOR IT!

THEY TRAVELED UP AND DOWN THE COAST, AND EVEN SPENT SOME TIME IN THE MIDWEST...

...MOSTLY ROBBING GAS STATIONS.

THAT WAS THE YEAR TRACY LEARNED HOW TO STEAL CARS...

...WHILE RICKY WAS BACK HOME, WATCHING THEIR MOTHER WASTE AWAY.

HE DIDN'T EVEN GET TO SAY GOODBYE. SHE'D BEEN DEAD FOR DAYS BY THE TIME HIS FATHER FOUND OUT.

AT THE FUNERAL, RICKY HIT TRACY IN THE FACE.

THE ONLY TIME HE EVER THREW THE FIRST PUNCH IN THEIR LIVES.

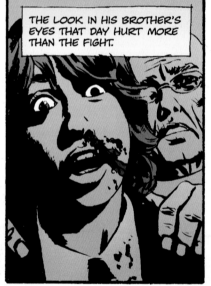

THE LOOK IN HIS BROTHER'S EYES THAT DAY HURT MORE THAN THE FIGHT.

TRACY THOUGHT HE GOT THE SHITTY END OF THE DEAL, TRAPPED IN CARS AND MOTEL ROOMS WITH THEIR FATHER.

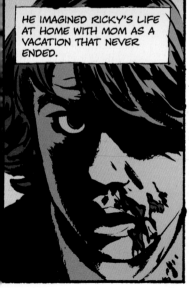

HE IMAGINED RICKY'S LIFE AT HOME WITH MOM AS A VACATION THAT NEVER ENDED.

INSTEAD THEY'D EACH BEEN TRAPPED IN THEIR OWN WORST NIGHTMARE.

IF ONLY YOU'D BEEN A COUPLE YEARS OLDER...

BRODERICK
LAWLESS
1972-2007
REST IN PEACE

IF ONLY YOUR LEGS WERE LONG ENOUGH TO REACH THE GAS PEDAL...

RICKY WOULD HAVE LOVED THAT YEAR WITH DAD.

AND TRACY COULD HAVE WITHSTOOD MOM'S SUFFERING, COULD HAVE COMFORTED HER.

...POOR KID... POOR FUCKING KID.

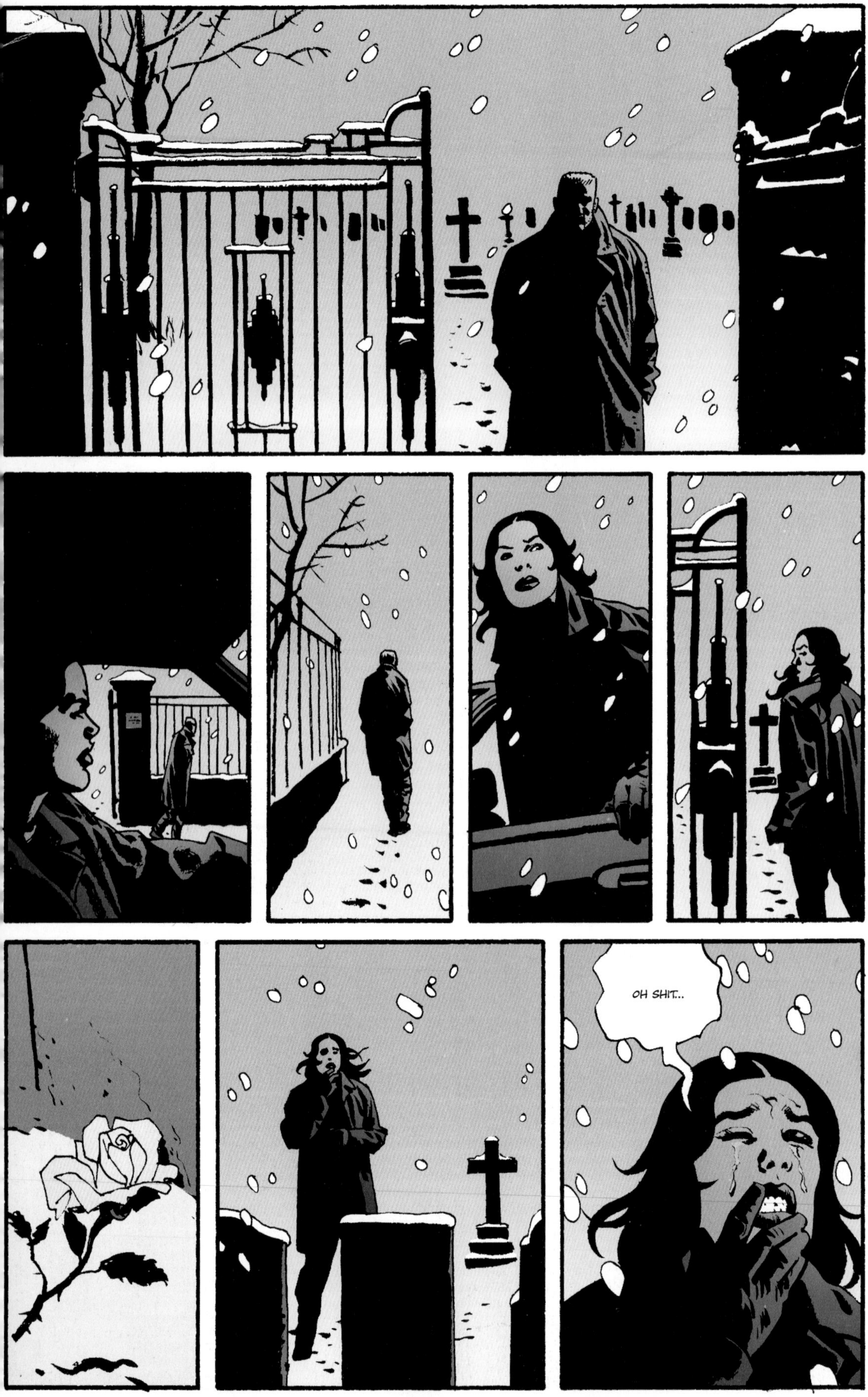
OH SHIT...

THERE WERE STILL TWO HOURS UNTIL THE MEET-UP BEFORE THE JOB.

BUT THE STREETS WERE MOSTLY DESERTED ALREADY, EXCEPT FOR A FEW LAST MINUTE SHOPPERS.

CHRISTMAS IN THE CITY FELT JUST AS EMPTY AS IT ALWAYS HAD.

HE WAS TIRED OF LIES... HE'D NEVER BEEN VERY GOOD AT THEM.

BUT ALL OF THAT WAS OVER OR WOULD BE SOON.

BECAUSE NO ONE WAS GOING TO BE IN TOUCH WITH SIMON UNTIL THE *SPLIT*...

...SO NO ONE WOULD MISS HIM.

OLD FUCKING PERV...

FINALLY, TRACY COULD ASK HIS QUESTIONS DIRECTLY.

STOP! PLEASE – YOU – YOU DON'T **HAVE** TO –

UHH!

FUCK, **CHESTER**... ENOUGH...

KNOW YOU MADE THIS SAM WEST FUCK'S **NEW I.D.**

EVEN THE **BOSS** RECOGNIZED YOUR WORK.

HE **KNOWS** YOU'RE HERE?

HE **SENT** YOU?!

TAKE IT EASY... TOLD ME NOT TO DO ANY **PERMANENT DAMAGE**...

THIS TIME.

LUCKY COINCIDENCE, US **LOOKIN'** FOR A GUY WHO STOLE SOME COUNTERFEIT MONEY... AN' **YOU** TURNIN' UP WITH A STACK.

OKAY... WHAT DO YOU **WANT** TO KNOW?

IT'S **SIMPLE**, JACOB... TELL ME WHO THE FUCK THIS BASTARD REALLY IS...

...AN' WHERE THE HELL I CAN FIND HIM.

BYE, SIMON... SEEYA TOMORROW...

FUCK'RE *YOU* DOING HERE, BOY?

NEED TO TALK TO YOU.

YOU'RE SUPPOSED TO BE GETTIN' *READY.*

THERE'S TIME.

WHAT IS THIS?

I WANT YOU TO TELL ME SOMETHING... WAS IT YOU --

-- WHO KILLED MY BROTHER?

...

Y'KNOW, I *THOUGHT* I RECOGNIZED YOU, I JUST...

NO.

AHH!

UHN!

I HAVE *NO PROBLEM* HURTING AN OLD MAN.

I FUCKIN' *NOTICED*...

BUT THIS DOESN'T *HAVE* TO GET UGLY... NECESSARILY.

SHIT... IT'S AS UGLY AS THEY GET, KID...

WHAT *ELSE* WOULD'JA CALL IT, WHAT YOU'RE DOIN'?

WHAT **I'M** DOING? I CAME HOME FOR ONE REASON... **RICKY'S KILLER.**

GOT A FUNNY WAY OF GOIN' ABOUT IT...

WALKIN' IN YOUR LITTLE BROTHER'S SHOES...

PUTTIN' YOUR COCK IN THE PUSSY HE CALLED HOME.

BUT RICKY WAS A TWISTED FUCK IN THE HEAD, TOO... JUST LIKE YOUR **DADDY**...

...WHY SHOULD **YOU** BE ANY DIFFERENT?

YOU LIKE TO **TALK**... KEEP IT UP.

FUCK YOU. NOT TELLIN' YOU **SHIT**, YOU BACK-STABBING FUCK.

YEAH, YOU WILL.

AND BEFORE IT WAS OVER, TRACY DID GET THE ANSWERS HE WANTED, AND A FEW HE **DIDN'T.**

BUT IT SEEMED TO HIM THAT WAS JUST THE NATURE OF ANSWERS.

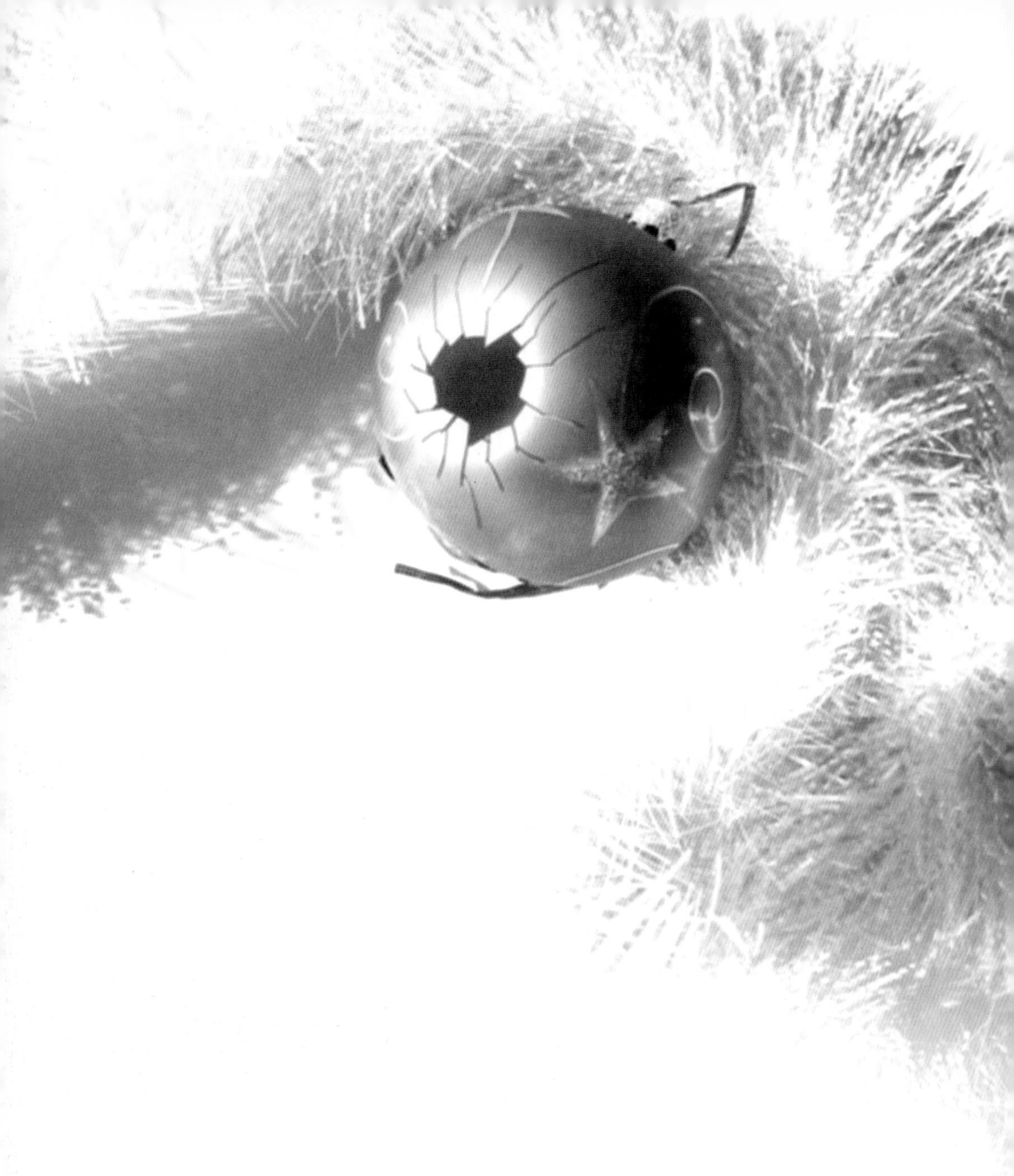

Part Five

THIS **TRACY LAWLESS** WAS GOING TO BE A SERIOUS PAIN IN THE ASS.

THAT'S WHAT CHESTER WAS THINKING AS HE DIALED THE BIG MAN'S NUMBER.

IT'S ME. I'M AT THE PLACE THEY **SAID**...

YEAH, HE'S HERE... AND HE AIN'T **GOIN'** ANYHERE.

GOT HIMSELF KILLED.

TOOK SOME **TIME** DOIN' IT, TOO... BROKEN FINGERS, THUMBS...

THIS WAS SOME NASTY-ASS **CAVEMAN** SHIT.

NAH, NOTHIN' IN HERE'S GONNA TELL ME WHAT THEIR **SCORE** IS...

UH HUNH... YEAH, BUT HOW MANY OPTIONS CAN THERE BE...?

...IT'S CHRISTMAS FUCKIN' **EVE.**

SIMON HAD BEEN PLANNING THIS HEIST FOR YEARS.

EVER SINCE HE'D FOUND OUT HOW MUCH CASH THE *SAINT DOMINIC'S CATHEDRAL* BLACK TIE *BENEFIT* USUALLY TOOK IN.

THIS *THOUSAND DOLLAR* PER PERSON EVENT HAD BECOME A FIXTURE AMONG THE CITY'S UPPER CLASS.

ALL DONATIONS WERE MADE *IN CASH*, WITH PROCEEDS SUPPOSEDLY GOING TO CAUSES IN AFRICA.

SO, THE IDLE RICH GOT THEIR PICTURE IN THE *SOCIETY PAGES* ON CHRISTMAS MORNING...

...*AND* GOT TO FEEL LIKE THEY WERE SAVING THE WORLD A LITTLE BIT.

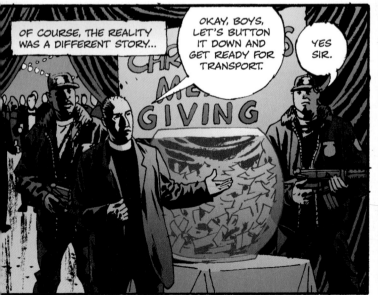

OF COURSE, THE REALITY WAS A DIFFERENT STORY...

OKAY, BOYS, LET'S BUTTON IT DOWN AND GET READY FOR TRANSPORT.

YES SIR.

...BECAUSE *FATHER BRIAN GRANT*, WHO RAN SAINT DOMINIC'S, WAS CROOKED AS HELL.

FOR DECADES HE'D BEEN SKIMMING *CHURCH TITHES* AND PUTTING THAT MONEY ON THE STREET.

LOANING IT TO 'POOR SOULS IN NEED.'

CHRISTMAS MEANS GIVING

AND JUST AS HE HAD NO PROBLEM WITH CORPORAL PUNISHMENT AT ST. DOMINIC'S SCHOOL...

...HE WASN'T OPPOSED TO HIS MEN BREAKING LEGS TO COLLECT DEBTS.

THEN HE'D COME UP WITH THE CHRISTMAS EVE *CASH-ONLY* BENEFIT...

AND REALIZED THAT THE RICH COULD BE EVEN EASIER TO FLEECE THAN THE POOR.

WITH THE POOR, YOU HAD TO *SELL* THE LIE TO GET THEM TO HAND OVER THEIR MONEY.

WITH THE RICH, YOU JUST NEEDED A LIE THEY WERE *WILLING* TO BELIEVE.

SO, ONCE THE PARTY WAS WELL UNDER WAY, THE EVENING'S PROCEEDS WERE TALLIED UP AND READIED FOR DEPOSIT...

...AND AN ARMORED TRANSPORT TOOK THE DEPOSIT TO A BANK DOWNTOWN.

FATHER GRANT MADE ARRANGEMENTS WITH THE MANAGER TO STAY LATE THAT NIGHT...

...WANTING TO ENSURE HIS CASH WAS SAFE IN A *VAULT* FOR THE CHRISTMAS HOLIDAY.

BECAUSE NO ONE IS MORE PARANOID ABOUT THEIR MONEY THAN A CRIMINAL.

THEY KNOW HOW *RARE* LARGE CASH SCORES HAVE BECOME IN THIS MODERN WORLD.

BUT THIS YEAR SIMON HAD A CONNECTION AT THE BANK, AND HAD BEEN TIPPED OFF TO THE SCHEDULED ARRIVAL OF THE ARMORED TRANSPORT.

IF THEY FOLLOWED HIS PLAN, THIS COULD BE ONE OF THE QUIETEST AND EASIEST HEISTS THEY'D EVER PULLED.

YOU READY?

OF COURSE I'M READY... I HAVE THE *BETTER* DISGUISE.

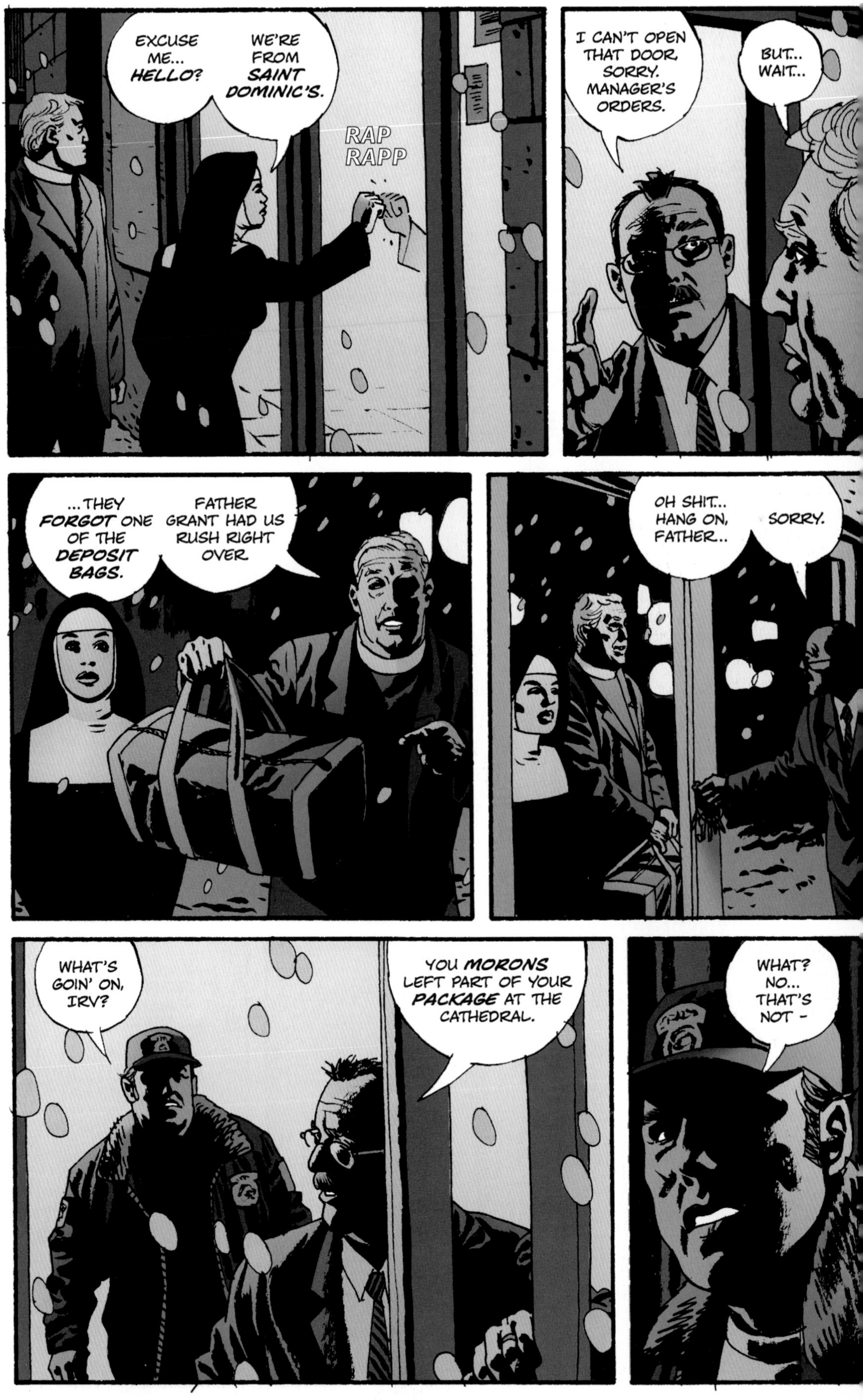

EXCUSE ME... HELLO?
WE'RE FROM SAINT DOMINIC'S.
RAP RAPP
I CAN'T OPEN THAT DOOR. SORRY. MANAGER'S ORDERS.
BUT... WAIT...
...THEY FORGOT ONE OF THE DEPOSIT BAGS.
FATHER GRANT HAD US RUSH RIGHT OVER
OH SHIT... HANG ON, FATHER...
SORRY.
WHAT'S GOIN' ON, IRV?
YOU MORONS LEFT PART OF YOUR PACKAGE AT THE CATHEDRAL.
WHAT? NO... THAT'S NOT -

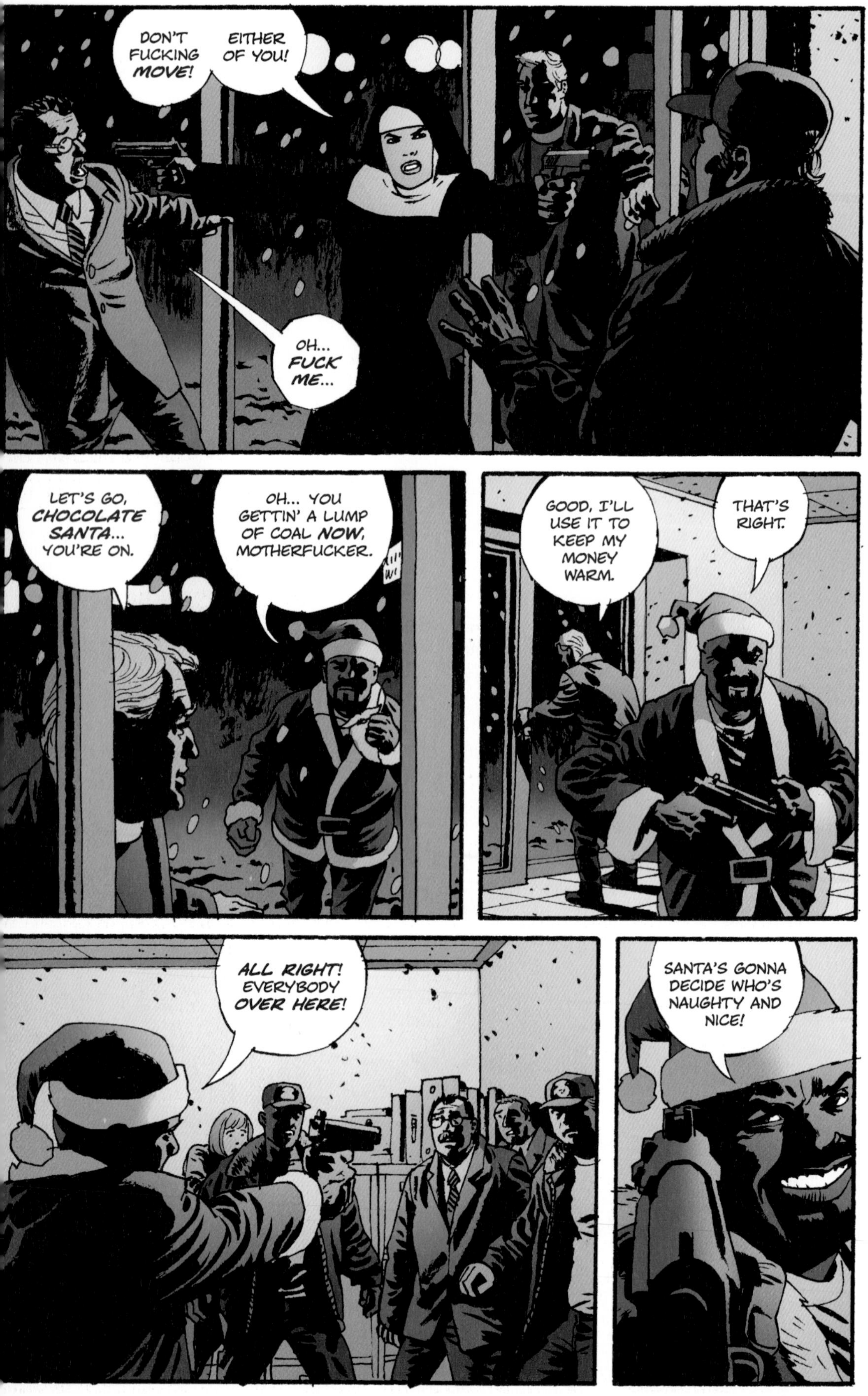
DON'T FUCKING MOVE!
EITHER OF YOU!
OH... FUCK ME...
LET'S GO, CHOCOLATE SANTA... YOU'RE ON.
OH... YOU GETTIN' A LUMP OF COAL NOW, MOTHERFUCKER.
GOOD, I'LL USE IT TO KEEP MY MONEY WARM.
THAT'S RIGHT.
ALL RIGHT! EVERYBODY OVER HERE!
SANTA'S GONNA DECIDE WHO'S NAUGHTY AND NICE!

TRACY WATCHED NELSON CONTROL THE BANK EMPLOYEES AND GUARDS...

...WHILE MALLORY AND GREY GATHERED THE DEPOSIT BAGS AND KEYS.

SIMON WAS RIGHT, THIS JOB WAS EVEN EASIER THAN IT LOOKED ON PAPER.

A SKELETON CREW IN THE BANK, A DESERTED CITY AROUND THEM.

TWO MINUTES OF RISK TO WALK AWAY WITH OVER HALF A MILLION, READY TO BE DIVIDED UP.

IT WOULD'VE ALL GONE PERFECTLY IF TRACY HADN'T CALLED 911 FOUR MINUTES AGO.

WHAT THE *FUCK*...?

GET IN!

HEY!

WHAT'RE YOU –

SKRREEEEEE

OH MY GOD – STOP.

AW... THIS IS NOT HAPPENING...

FREEZE! DON'T EVEN *BREATHE*, MOTHERFUCKERS!

FUCK IT.

JESUS!

YOU FUCKER! BASTARD!

SHUT UP.

PIECE OF SHIT! YOU DIDN'T –

SHUT UP.

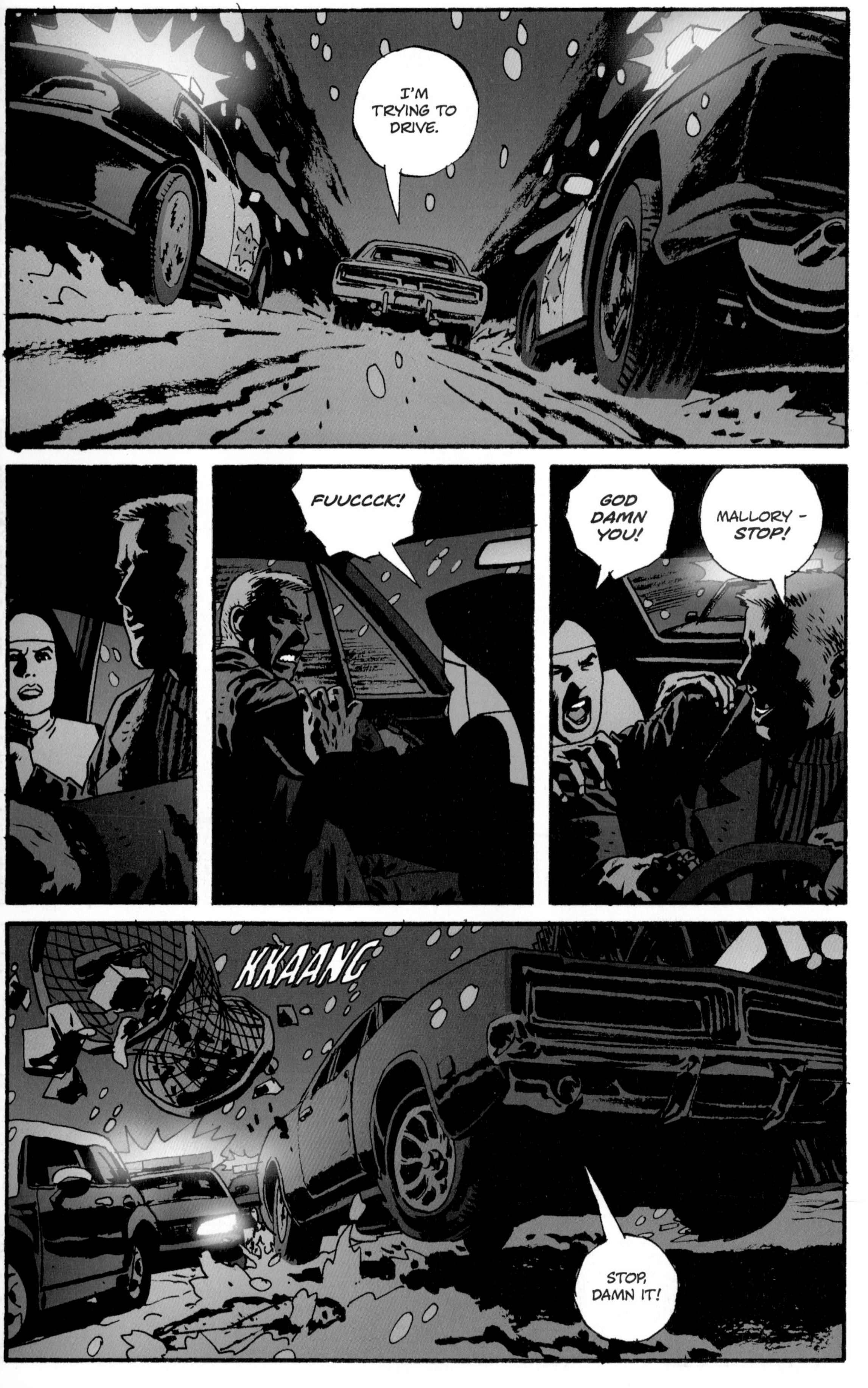
I'M TRYING TO DRIVE.
FUUCCCK!
GOD DAMN YOU!
MALLORY - STOP!
KKAANG
STOP, DAMN IT!

ENOUGH!

JUST SIT STILL...

--REPEAT, OFFICERS NEED **ASSISTANCE.** SUSPECT VEHICLE –

-- FLEEING SOUTH ON BORDEN TOWARDS GOSSAMER...

YOU DIDN'T HAVE TO DO THAT TO THEM... BASTARD.

AND YOU BARELY GOT ANY OF THE SCORE.

LIKE I GIVE A SHIT... *MOVE.*

SO, THIS IS YOUR BIG PLAN?

ALL THAT HARD WORK... JUST TO SET US UP?

I'M DISAPPOINTED, *TRACY.*

THAT'S RIGHT. I *FOLLOWED* YOU TODAY.

TO THE GRAVEYARD.

BUT YOU DIDN'T TELL GREY... OR SKIP OUT ON THE JOB.

WHY NOT?

WHY DO YOU FUCKING *THINK?!*

SO... DO YOU KNOW WHAT THIS PLACE IS?

YEAH. AN EMPTY FUCKING SHELL... JUST LIKE YOU.

RICKY USED TO COME OUT HERE SOMETIMES, TOO... WHEN HE WAS DRUNK...

THE LAWLESS FAMILY HOME...

A SHITHOLE IN SOME FORGOTTEN SLUM.

SO, ARE YOU GONNA DO IT OR NOT?

I WANT TO HEAR IT FROM YOUR MOUTH... THE TRUTH.

AND I WANNA KNOW WHY.

YOU THINK IT'S THAT SIMPLE?

YOU DIDN'T EVEN KNOW HIM.

JUST TELL ME.

DON'T MAKE ME HURT YOU, MALLORY.

BECAUSE THIS HAS BEEN SO PAINLESS UNTIL NOW, RIGHT?

Your brother never had any trouble hurting me. He **never** minded hurting **anyone**, really. I think that was what I liked about him at First.

Ricky Lawless... Hard as hell and twice as much trouble.

But he had **something** in him, buried deep... that no one but me could see. Something Fragile. A **sweetness**, almost.

It made what we had **mean** something. Like there was some **secret** to us that no one else knew about.

Except, the more he let me see that side... The meaner he'd get when he was drinking. I'm a big girl, though. It wasn't the First time a man hit me.

But with Ricky, I somehow felt... not like it was my fault... but not *blameless* either, you know? Was he self-destructing *because* of me?

And when he hit me, all I saw was that scared little kid inside... And I felt sorry for *him*.

I know that's crazy, but it's what kept me coming back to him... And trying to stop him from destroying himself and everything in his life.

Then last year, Ricky and Simon starting going at it over *everything* and I knew worse times were coming.

The night of the Tramwell heist, I knew he was in trouble... He'd screwed up some deal, but I had no idea how far he'd go.

He was going to take the whole score and run for it... leave town. But he knew Grey and Simon would come after him, even over eighty grand, so he was going to take care of them before he left.

When I tried to stop him, he practically knocked me out.

Still probably saved Grey's life, 'cause Rick was in such a rage he just beat the hell out of him instead of shooting him.

I was pretty out of it for a few minutes, but the next thing I remember is his voice, telling me to get in the car.

WHAT? YOU'RE BRINGING ME WITH YOU?

'COURSE YOU'RE COMING... I LOVE YOU.

And that was what did it, I guess.

BLAM

I just couldn't take that kind of love anymore.

EVEN I'M NOT THAT CRAZY... IT WAS JUST... NEVER GOING TO END.

AND I DON'T KNOW *WHAT* YOUR PARENTS OR THOSE FUCKERS IN *JUVIE* DID TO HIM... BUT HE WAS JUST TOO DAMAGED.

HE HATED HIMSELF TOO MUCH.

BUT YOU... HE CARRIED AROUND THAT LITTLE *HALF-PICTURE* OF YOU. TOLD ME ALL ABOUT HIS *BIG BROTHER*.

THE ARMY BADASS. TOUGHEST GUY IN THE WORLD.

I'D HAVE BEEN DISAPPOINTED IF YOU *HADN'T* SHOWN UP.

AND NOW YOU KNOW. IT WASN'T *ANY* OF THEM... IT WAS *ME*.

I *ALREADY* KNEW. SIMON TOLD ME.

SIMON? JESUS... YOU'RE *SOME* AVENGING ANGEL.

KILLING ALL THE *WRONG* PEOPLE.

WELL, GO AHEAD THEN... FUCKING *DO IT.* GET THE RIGHT PERSON, TOO.

I *DESERVE* IT.

GET OUT OF HERE, MALLORY.

WHAT...?

JUST... FUCKING *GO...* BEFORE I CHANGE MY MIND...

YOU'RE A BASTARD.

I KNOW.

THE PAST CALLS FROM THE SHADOWS AS HE STANDS AMONG THESE WALLS.

HIS BROTHER'S LAUGHTER, HIS MOTHER'S SCREAMS, HIS FATHER'S SILENCE... ALL KNOTTED TOGETHER, ECHOING ACROSS TIME.

AND HE KNOWS HE SHOULD NEVER HAVE COME BACK HERE.

HEY MAN... JUST BE COOL.

MAARRAAAW! MRRKK!

NOW, I KNOW YOU'RE A REAL HARD CASE, TRACY...

BUT I PROMISE I CAN PUT A BULLET IN HER BEFORE YOU DO SHIT.

DON'T.

UP TO YOU. GOT A MAN NEEDS TO SEE YOU.

COME ALONG NICELY... SHE LIVES.

FINE. LET'S GO.

THIS GUY IS GOOD, TRACY THINKS. KEEPS A COOL HEAD. KNOWS HOW TO CONTROL A SITUATION.

HE TAKES MALLORY, AND MAKES TRACY FOLLOW IN HIS CAR. KNOWS TRACY WON'T MAKE A FALSE MOVE WHILE SHE'S AT RISK.

WHICH MEANS THEY KNOW ABOUT HIM. ALL ABOUT HIM.

...TWENTY SEVEN MEN *MURDERED* IN BOSNIA... WHAT IS THE NAME OF THIS VILLAGE?

JARUGE.

THOSE MEN WERE RUNNING A *CAMP.*

SO IT *SAYS* IN YOUR FILE. BUT WHAT ABOUT THE THREE *U.S. SOLDIERS* KILLED IN BAGHDAD?

THAT PART HAS BEEN *REDACTED* HERE.

HE'D BEEN TOO LATE. THAT WAS THE TRAGEDY. TOO LATE TO DO ANYTHING BUT KILL.

THE GIRL HAD BEEN SAVED, OF COURSE... BUT JUST FROM THE FIRE.

HER FAMILY LAY DEAD IN THE DIRT, HER LIFE IN RUINS.

...I'M SORRY...

TRACY WAS THROWN IN A HOLE WHILE THE HIGHER-UPS TRIED TO BURY YET ANOTHER DISASTER IN IRAQ.

IT WAS ONE THING TO LOOK THE OTHER WAY ON WHAT HE'D DONE IN BOSNIA... BUT WHEN *U.S. SOLDIERS* WERE INVOLVED...

...THEN IT WAS ABOUT MORE THAN RIGHT AND WRONG. THEN IT WAS ABOUT PERCEPTION.

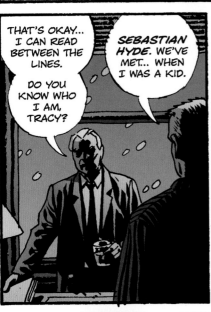

THAT'S OKAY... I CAN READ BETWEEN THE LINES.

DO YOU KNOW WHO I AM, TRACY?

SEBASTIAN HYDE. WE'VE MET... WHEN I WAS A KID.

GOOD MEMORY.

YOU *COST ME* THESE PAST WEEKS, KID. *PRESTIGE* MOSTLY, BUT STILL...

THAT MONEY YOU TOOK WAS A *SAMPLE DELIVERY* FROM A NEW SUPPLIER.

IMAGINE HOW I *LOOK* TO THEM NOW... IT'S EMBARRASSING.

HOW DID YOU FIND ME?

WHEN YOU'RE DRIVING A GETAWAY CAR, DON'T TAKE IT *HOME.* EVEN TO AN *OLD* HOME.

'CAUSE THERE'S ALWAYS A CHANCE SOMEONE'S GONNA KNOW WHO YOU *REALLY* ARE.

SOMEONE LIKE CHESTER, MY FRIEND WHO'S WATCHING YOUR LADY.

YOU CAN LET HER GO NOW.

I DON'T THINK SO. NOT YET.

YOU WANT *ME*, NOT HER. I'M THE ONE THAT WRONGED YOU.

YOU CAME BACK BECAUSE OF YOUR *BROTHER*? BECAUSE HE DIED?

WHAT DO YOU THINK?

I THINK FAMILY IS A *TRAP*... BUT I FIGURE YOU ALREADY KNOW THAT...

...OR YOU WOULDN'T BE HOME FOR CHRISTMAS WITH THE DEAD.

AND YOU WOULDN'T BE SO READY TO JOIN THEM.

YOU'RE *NOT* PLANNING TO KILL ME?

NOT NOW THAT I KNOW WHO YOU *ARE*. NO.

WHAT DO YOU *WANT* THEN?

WELL, YOUR BROTHER OWED ME A LOT OF MONEY. AND LOOKING AT YOUR MILITARY FILE...

I COULDN'T HELP BUT THINK, SKILLS LIKE YOURS...

...I COULD REALLY *USE* A MAN LIKE THAT.

SO HE MADE A DEAL. HE'D WORK FOR HYDE, JUST AS HIS FATHER ONCE HAD, AND MALLORY WOULDN'T BE HARMED...

TAKE IT.

GO TO HELL.

TAKE IT, MAL... IT'S EVERYTHING LEFT FROM THE SCORE. YOU'LL NEED IT.

SMAK

REVENGE. THAT'S WHAT HE HAD COME HOME FOR... BUT IT DIDN'T REALLY EXIST, DID IT?

JUST EMPTY REGRET AND BITTER HEARTBREAK WANDERING THE STREETS.

THE CITY AROUND HIM, WHITE AND GREY AND COLD, FELT SUDDENLY SO SMALL.

HEY MAN -- MERRY CHRISTMAS... MEEERRRY CHRISTMASSS!!!

HYDE HAD BEEN RIGHT ABOUT FAMILY, THERE WAS NO ESCAPING IT...

HA HAHA HA...

...EVEN WHEN THERE WAS NO ONE LEFT TO RUN FROM.

The End

Brubaker Phillips Staples

For My Brother

ALSO AVAILABLE: **Criminal Vol. 1: COWARD**

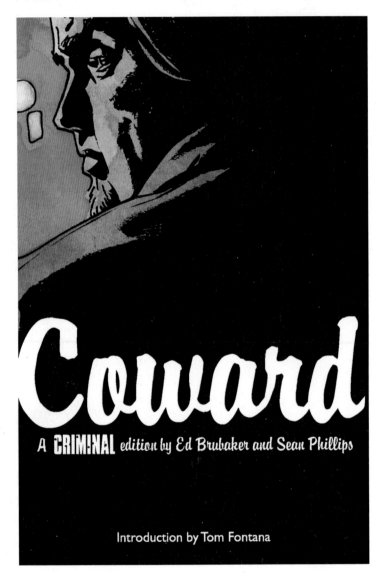